Salt

**Selected Stories
and Essays**

ALSO BY BRUCE PASCOE

A Corner Full of Characters, Blackstone Press (1981)

Night Animals, Penguin Books (1986)

Fox, McPhee Gribble/Penguin Books (1988)

Ruby-eyed Coucal, Magabala Books (1996)

Wathaurong: Too Bloody Strong: Stories and Life Journeys of People from Wathaurong, Pascoe Publishing (1997)

Shark, Magabala Books (1999)

Nightjar, Seaglass Books (2000)

Earth, Magabala Books (2001)

Ocean, Bruce Sims Books (2002)

Foxies in a Firehose: A Piece of Doggerel from Warragul, Seaglass Books (2006)

Convincing Ground: Learning to Fall in Love with Your Country, Aboriginal Studies Press (2007)

The Little Red Yellow Black Book: An Introduction to Indigenous Australia, Aboriginal Studies Press (2008)

Bloke, Penguin Books (2009)

Fog a Dox, Magabala Books (2012)

Dark Emu: Black Seeds: Agriculture or Accident?, Magabala Books (2014)

Seahorse, Magabala Books (2015)

Mrs Whitlam, Magabala Books (2016)

Salt

Selected Stories
and Essays

BRUCE PASCOE

Published by Black Inc.,
an imprint of Schwartz Books Pty Ltd
Level 1, 221 Drummond Street
Carlton VIC 3053, Australia
enquiries@blackincbooks.com
www.blackincbooks.com

9781760641580 (paperback)
9781743821053 (ebook)

A catalogue record for this
book is available from the
National Library of Australia

Cover design by Akiko Chan
Cover photograph by Vicky Shukuroglou
Text design and typesetting by Akiko Chan
Ant holes on p. viii by Thaanawatkaewsri/Shutterstock; Coral fungi on pp. 54–5
by Full Tank/Shutterstock; Underwater plant on pp. 102–3 by Steve Lovegrove/
Shutterstock; Tree on pp. 138–9 by Mark Higgins/Shutterstock; Desert/snow
plant on pp. 200–1 by Joachim Heng/Shutterstock; Rivergum trunk on
pp. 266–7 by Kingropes Access/Shutterstock

Printed in Australia by McPherson's Printing Group.

for the three salt rivers of Mallacoota

CONTENTS

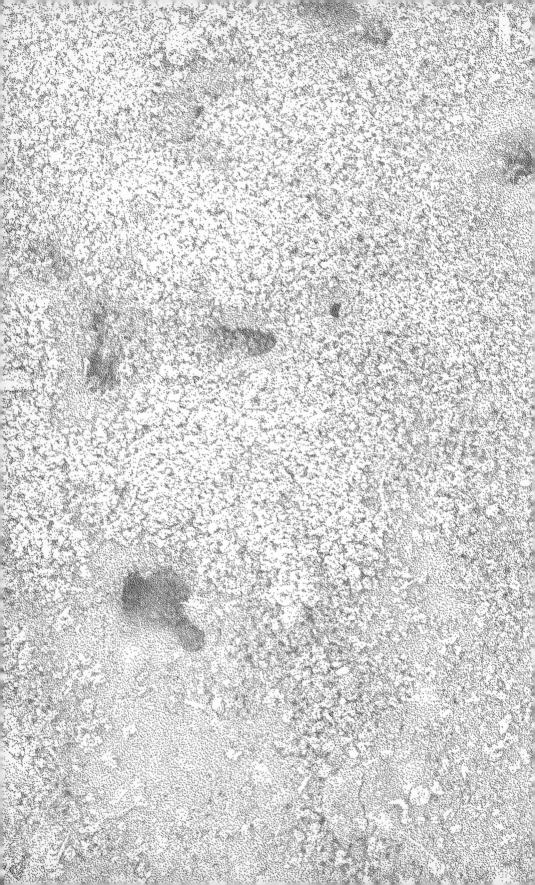

COUNTRY

A LETTER TO BARRY

Why did I think of you when I saw the fox hunting mullet in the river shallows? She must have been engrossed in her work because her coat was damp and she'd ruffled it into feathers to protect herself from the cold. Her back was hunched as she stepped gingerly through the slip of water on the sandbar. Tea-tree tannin had steeped the river in amber, and you couldn't help admiring the dark ginger fox on a ground of golden liquor.

The only awkward posture in the scene was the way she hunched – whether as reaction to the cold or coiled to pounce on fish, I couldn't tell. She didn't seem pleased by my sudden appearance but refused to look at me directly. The insouciance of vixens.

She would endure my presence simply because she was unwilling to waste the investment in her hunt. I was hunting too and knew how she felt: the intensity, the coiled energy, the hope.

I felt guilty for having imposed on her radiant quest. I passed on the opposite side of the river, guiding the boat through the shallow channel that hugged the melaleucas and wattles growing on the bank. I looked back at her when I could take my eye from the navigation, fascinated by her high-stepping stealth.

And I thought of you. Once again it took me days to return your call, and you probably think I'm rude or neglectful, but I try to avoid the telephone, as you know, and my attention is so thoroughly in debt to the river, the insistence of its life.

The mist was thick at dawn. It hung like the gauze curtains you see in the back rooms of some old hotels where any welcome is reserved for the public areas. The forgotten rooms where guests would stay in more prosperous times are left to decay, to shred, to dream old tattered dreams. The river mist wreathed in frayed drifts like that grey gauze of disappointment.

I had to peer into those old shabby rooms to find the river banks and the landmarks I used to follow the channel in the sandy river's course. At last I could make out old Geoff's fence. He shot himself last year. I wish he hadn't. Took it bad when he had to sell the farm. The town blamed her but I'd seen them only a month before he died. Fishing together. They seemed happy. But how can you tell? Was the fox insouciant or careless? I chose the pride of insouciance because I was just an observer, as distant from the true workings of a fox's brain as I was from the motivations of most humans. Just an intrigued observer. No gift other than curiosity.

I loved Geoff. When I returned prodigal to the rivers after twenty-five years away, Geoff was delighted to see me and I clung to his welcome. He sat me down to remind me of a cricket game we'd played together thirty-two years ago.

Geoff loved his cricket, and loved talking about his two-game career. In Geoff's version of events his contribution was vivid – not overly embellished, but his ordinariness was central to the play. It was a great way to be welcomed.

I wish you hadn't done it, Geoff. I can't bear to look at your hillsides now.

Then I passed Byron's farm. He was a city man, a nerve nut, nose eroded by alcohol. He decided to become a market gardener but the tomato wilt got him. Though really it was the absence of his wife. She couldn't stand the loneliness of the river, the dawn mists parting reluctantly like the shrouds in a funeral parlour. Byron couldn't explain its beauty and she couldn't bear the awful screaming of the yellow-bellied glider, the haunting white ghostliness of the masked owl. And its call: like death itself.

Byron grieved and so, after another year of battling the wilt, he left the hothouses and went back to the suburbs. For love.

And the next farm, on the bluff above Byron's empty gardens, belongs to a Samoan abalone diver. His brother was shot by a gay man who had no other answer for the derision he was dealt. The surviving brother played one game of cricket just so he could use his dead brother's bat. Geoff would have loved it. So did I. I taught both brothers. Wild men of the sea, lovely lost Samoans. And the other man is out of prison now and he's still lost.

The mist still obscured the landmarks and I peered through its veils to find the sandy beach that marked a treacherous bend. A mate saved a kid's life there when he cut the fishing line tangled around a toddler's leg. The other end was attached to an eighty-pound mulloway heading for Bass Strait. That toddler's father later sold the riverbank farm to Phillip, a man who made his fortune recovering swamplands in the environmental eighties. The river community hated him for allowing the salt water to resume its old course across the paddocks. Old Geoff didn't like it either, and sawed off the two giant ironbark gateposts, which Phillip used to block the communal roadway. Well, Geoff thought it was communal; Phillip thought it was his land. Geoff sawed his posts off and told me of his act of defiance with enormous glee. He even rubbed his hands together as he retold the story as if he was in some rural cartoon.

Geoff was dead now and Phillip was ill, but it was Phillip who had taken in Geoff's ancient blind terrier, Mate, after Geoff died. Funny world.

Phillip was combative, but he would say assertive. He did not get along with the abalone diver across the river. Being a fisherman, Dean liked fast boats, even though one of them was a yacht.

I loved seeing that yacht on the river. Phillip saw a fast boat.

And their upstream neighbour was Marion. Some of Marion's partners weren't evidence of her ability to make good choices. One of her men set himself alight after an argument as I happened to be leaving the hotel adjoining her house. I saw all Marion's kids, including one I didn't know she had, vaulting the fence. I had taught them all except the one who'd escaped education completely. No homework to be handed in tomorrow, I thought as the house burnt down.

But she was a great person, Marion, full of life and cheek. I was surprised when she moved in with Col, but on more thorough consideration it was her most inspired choice.

Col was a Jackson of Jacksons Bridge, and his family had held the farm since it was first cleared. Some said the Jacksons had Aboriginal blood, but that claim could be levelled at most of the district families who could trace their inheritance back three or four generations. It was a lonely river. My great-grandfather got lonely too, but on a different river.

Col played in those golden cricket games that were so vivid in Geoff's memory. But Col was even worse than Geoff, although he was the best horseman in East Gippsland. Col indulged his cattle's roaming personalities just so he had an excuse to ride through the mountains looking for them. He never built a fence in his life, preferring to ride into New South Wales or up into the Alps to retrieve his esteemed line of crossbred duffers. Ayrshire being among the sires. My Ayrshire, my broken fence. Thanks, Col.

If you're chasing your cattle, and those of farmers less attentive to stock control, across a couple of state borders you need good dogs. Col had about thirty mixed-breed border-collie-kelpie-dingo-beagles. Bad dogs. Savage, independent, bloody near feral mongrels. Col's cattle-breeding techniques were also applied to the refinement of his cattle dogs' pedigree.

I was milking one misty morning. That old river mist was a river in itself and we got it in all seasons. Even as high up as my farm on the Maramingo, a wilder tributary of the wild Jinnor just before it joins the Wallagaraugh. It was breathtaking to watch the stealthy grey steal entire mountains from your gaze only to reveal them a moment later – a flick of the magician's wrist.

My jersey, Milly, was a darling cow and let me press my face into her loin while I milked her. We had an agreement about the amount of milk I could take before she'd stamp her foot to remind me the rest was for her calf.

But this particular morning of funereal mist she swung her head to look down into the valley long before we'd reached the point of agreed shares. I peered beneath her steaming belly and could see these mongrel wild dogs. Two, three, six … Jesus, nine. Col. He must have been doing one of his interstate stocktaking visits, or bringing his cattle on a raid to my Ayrshire bull. Thanks, Col.

On an earlier occasion, I had docked my old open clinker on Col's beach beside the bridge so I could remove the Simplex engine and take it to be repaired by Larry Blair. But don't start me on the Blairs. When I turned up to re-install the motor, *Nadgee* was no longer there. She was dubbed *Nadgee* by Doug Barrow senior, who sailed her down the coast from Narooma and surfed her across the bar into the Mallacoota lakes. The Barrows were one of those wild early families, and their forefathers had overlanded from Sydney across the Alps to Bombala in 1832. I had bought a bed off old Doug once and on the back of the bedhead was scrawled in chalk *Barrow, Bombala, 1834*. It was an ugly bed but I kept it for the chalk of Australian history. But don't start me on the Barrows, either.

The important thing was that *Nadgee* was gone. I enquired of Col as to the boat's location. 'Gawn,' he said, 'in the flood.' A week previous we'd had a few centimetres of rain – not enough to take a styrofoam cup off the bank. I wondered how much Col's river-side enterprises benefited from the disappearance of the clinker.

Did I say I wasn't going to start on the Blairs? Well, you can't talk about the river without mentioning them. When Larry Blair's wife, May, left him, she took up residence with a very peculiar man in a very peculiar caravan on the opposite bank of the river from where she was born as a member of the Jacksons of Jackson's Bridge. She said Larry was mean and had individualised the meaning of the marriage contract. The caravan was her way of returning to the seat of the family estate.

Larry was an old fisherman turned boat-hire magnate and lived in a broken wooden house on a green bank of the lower lake. He knew everything there was to know about the Simplex engine. He could fix the magneto by putting it beside his wood stove.

Worked a treat. Blocked fuel lines, seized pistons – he had a rural solution for each problem. Except marriage.

He looked most of all like Steptoe from *Steptoe and Son*, and had a wheedling little voice and licked his lips and hunched his shoulders whenever he spoke so that it felt like a conspiracy whenever he talked to you about the weather or a cow with mastitis. I thought May was right.

The German baker said that Larry would never have the right change for his bread; he'd always be short. The baker kept a book. Larry never paid. The baker never forgot. May was right.

Above Jackson's Bridge old Simmonds had a farm where he boiled down wallabies and dead chooks for his pigs. Local women used to have Christmas parties on the farm where they bounced around naked, so it was rumoured. Everybody has to let their hair down once in a while.

And above the captain's block was old Burgess. I never knew him, only saw him once in a boat he was rowing upstream with the crudest pair of mismatched oars I'd ever seen.

Burgess would never go into town. He'd leave anonymous parcels of fish on people's back steps at dawn, and they'd leave groceries and grog on his. The secret transactions of the unseen. Fair proportion of grog in the groceries.

When I had arrived as a teacher in the seventies, all the river people told me the original teacher used to row a long skiff as far upstream as Burgess's to teach all the river kids. This was long before Burgess arrived, of course, but that teacher's students were the Jacksons and Blairs and Barrows and Donaldsons. Wild kids. No shoes, no interest, but the best ship handlers on the east coast of the continent.

Across the river from Burgess was Bobby Nicholls, who had married a local Yuin woman. I regretted selling my tractor to Bobby. I had bought it from Robert Arnot's father, who farmed on the New South Wales end of the river, above the highway. The Arnots were an old, old family from Timbillica, and the tractor I bought was the old man's first, and he parted with it like he knew his life as a real man was over. From now on he'd be a man who didn't farm.

I remembered harvesting hay with him a year before he gave the farm to his son. It was a hot day in December and we were using ancient steel-tined hay forks to pitch mown hay onto a wooden cart that the old man towed behind the tractor to a shed with slatted walls. Old Man Arnot's father had built that shed to dry corn; it was one of the first farm structures in the entire district. If you didn't count the thatched houses of Aborigines. Which, of course, no one did. We pitched hay all day, the old man and I, in grim silence. He was one of those quiet country gentlemen, but that was not the cause of his silence; he just resented that I was young and he was old.

The tractor I had bought was a hundred years more recent than the shed, but it was still old. A Fordson Major petrol-kero model – you had to start it with kerosene before switching over to petrol. It was a beast, could pull anything, drag the stumps of old trees straight out of the ground as if they were pensioners' teeth. I loved it. My daughter did too, and had insisted on riding behind me. No roll bar, not many brakes, and when I thought of that little red-haired girl riding between those giant wheels I shuddered. Tractors and wild river children.

Anyway, I sold it to Bobby Nicholls. In a hurry. I'd split up with the girl's mother and the farm had to be sold. Probably the reason why Geoff killed himself. No regard for himself without the farm.

But what Bobby Nicholls did to that tractor really upset Robert, old Robert Arnot's son, because it had been his father's pride and joy. The Arnots had arrived in Australia to go whaling with Ben Boyd. They were proud of their history and prouder of their tractors. Bobby Nicholls was a humourless fundamentalist Christian, and he oxy-torched three inches off each side of the tractor's grader blade so it would fit onto his trailer. The act of a heathen, Robert believed.

The Arnots were family of mine. My son-in-law's grandmother was Jean Arnot of Wangarabell. How could such remote acts of chance occur on such a lonely river?

At the top of the river on the day of the fox, I caught my fish from a snag I'd last fished six years earlier with Robert's brother-in-law, Kevin, two weeks before he died of a heart attack. I couldn't fish that river without thinking of Kevin, or Geoff, or my tractor, or Larry Blair's funny way of talking.

And I thought of you, mate, when I saw the fox – not because you remind me of a fox, but because as soon as I saw such a strange thing I wondered who would be interested in the story. Do all people do that as they watch an event unfold, or is it just us, the storytellers?

Coming back down the river I kept a lookout for the fox. She was still there, hunkered down on the sandspit. As I had passed the first time I noticed a plover sitting on eggs on the downstream end of the sand island and thought it typical fox behaviour to sneak out onto the sand and outlast the plover's indignation. This time, two dotterels were running backward and forwards just metres from the fox's nose, desperate to distract attention from their young. They must have had a nest there too.

I watched the fox to see if it would react. I cast a line to make the sinker splash as close to the animal as I could manage. I saw the ears twitch to the sound, but it showed no other reaction. Cunning bastard, I thought, pretending it's not there. Typical fox.

So I stepped out of my boat, *Nadgee III,* and waded to the island. I saw the ears rotate towards the sound of my steps.

There was a good boondie on the sand and I picked it up, not willing to be attacked by a cornered fox. It got to its feet and faced me, swaying slightly before it tottered and almost fell, still trying to look defiant and strong. But it wasn't strong; it was a sick fox. If it was fishing for mullet, this was the act of a desperate animal, not the invention of artful adaption. The expenditure of energy in becoming wet and cold could hardly justify the potential catch. No, this was just a sick fox, probably bleeding to death from ingesting a fox bait, which are almost pure warfarin, the haemorrhaging agent with which we poison rats.

The golden eyes could barely focus, but she knew my intent. She avoided the first swing of the club by the merest turn of her head, but I collected it with the returning pendulum and cracked that fine skull. Blood gushed from its ears and nose. The warfarin was already well into its work.

I returned to my boat burdened with sorrow. I'd misjudged her with my prejudice, even inclining towards admiration for fox cunning and innovation instead of reading her actions for what they were, dying movements. We're meant to kill foxes, but are we meant to cause them such slow agony? And her teats were hanging, too. Was there more agony to come? Cubs slowly succumbing to a starving sleep. As I succumbed to my own sleeplessness, estranged from the sleeper beside me.

So, I bought the old farm where Geoff shot himself. I got rid of the stained carpet and patched the 22-millimetre hole in the ceiling. I now sit beside Geoff's fire with my two dogs bookending my knees as I dream of foxes, wild red-haired girls, fish and starvation.

I'm sorry not to visit you more, old mate, sorry to be tardy in the mere return of a phone call, but the river is such a demanding home. She insists you bear witness. As you have just done.

REAPING SEEDS
OF DISCONTENT

We were stranded on a heathland west of Shipwreck Creek like an unhappy family of arthritic brolgas. Our mission had been to find a rare banksia, and our success had been achieved so quickly we were faced with the prospect of returning before we'd even popped the plugs on our battered vacuum flasks.

We stood there surveying the scene of our triumph in doleful exhilaration. We were boffins mostly, so the emotion came as easily to us as our woeful choice of tailors.

One of the thrill-seekers swept his cap across the tops of the grass. He'd received the hat during a Bi-Lo grocery-chain promotion; you can't look a free cap in the peak, so it had become part of his ensemble.

'What's this?' he hooted mournfully as we all looked into his cap, wishing it was us who'd been there the day Bi-Lo went mad with generosity. It was full of seed.

'*Themeda triandra*,' another of the thrill-seekers murmured. 'Kangaroo grass.'

The brolgas moved on, planning a grand celebration of thermos coffee on the beach. I dawdled behind them, not wanting to get

involved too early in the shenanigans, and repeated Bi-Lo's action
with my own cap, found on the river bank after the 2009 flood.

My hat was full of seed, too, and I looked around at the uniform height of the grass heads. Growing through the heath and
banksia was a monoculture of kangaroo grass, all the same height
and nearly all maturing its seed at the same time. If twenty of you
stretched out in line with, let's say, coolamons, you could harvest
this 200-acre field in three or four days.

That's too much seed to eat all at once, but if you milled the
grain and stored the flour you could eat it later. Giles and Mitchell
had found such stores on their Australian explorations, Gregory
had seen fields being sowed and irrigated, and Sturt had witnessed
the grinding process.

I've been walking this heath since 1974 looking for orchids,
tawny-crowned honeyeaters, banksias, ground parrots and the sort
of stuff that interests people who wear second-hand hats. I should
have noticed this grass before, should have wondered why it was
so predominant, why it was seeding all at once. But I didn't. I'd
been educated in Australia, where we train our minds not to think
of stuff like that, preferring instead to be excited by rare sightings
of a dull green parrot.

The white history of Australia is so pervasive, and laden so
thoroughly with warm platitudes of self-congratulation, that the
image of the Australian as a good-natured knockabout humourist
has seeded our literature and society. The effect is so comprehensive that any questioning of the national character is met with
incredulity, followed by venom. The letters pages of all national
newspapers were whipped into a froth of indignation once when
it was suggested in a school curriculum that Australia was invaded

rather than settled. We like the word 'settled' for its benign passivity.

I swallowed that history hook, line and sinker, but the gruff teachings and questions of the Elders eroded that confidence. I began to question everything, especially those things Australians claimed to know about Australia. We had just walked through a field of harvest, but a field where the harvesters had been discouraged from their labour 170 years ago. Discouraged by murder.

The image of the hat full of grain stayed with me. And when at last I began to investigate the real Aboriginal economy so frankly described by the explorers, I remembered the ugly hat. I'd been growing murnong tubers for five years by then, and the Barkindji, Latji Latji and Mutti Mutti had shown me how to make bread from *Panicum decompositum* in the sand dunes of Lake Mungo.

I went back to the heathland, eschewing the charms of parrots and obscure banksia, and stripped the heads of the *Themeda triandra*. I posted the grain to a mate whose edgy glee comes from milling the seed of grasses. I knew the first time I met him that he knew what he was doing because he was still driving his mother-in-law's 1986 Mercedes that gloried in a dashboard cracked like a surfer's lips and decorated by enough tartan rugs to keep the Highlands happy for a decade.

Uncle Mercedes produced 500 grams of wholemeal flour and 200 of more refined flour from three kilograms of seed heads. The flour was dark but smelt like a late summer field at dusk, earthy and warm, and tasted rich and fruity. But this old man was of such natural innocence that he spread it on a coffee table and began to separate it with a pencil. I looked about for the narcotics police, but old Mercedes was lost in concentration as he marvelled at what had been elicited from unfashionable grain. Too crude, too small, too Australian.

Next day, my wife, Lyn, the only orchid boffin I know who can walk into a bush paddock looking like Shelley Ware from *The Marngrook Footy Show,* blended the *Themeda* flour with white flour and combined them with her starter yeast and baked a loaf of bread. I was nervous. I chewed a corner off the loaf, and my heart leapt. It was beautiful and had the unmistakable perfume and flavour of the kangaroo grass.

We had bread of exceptional taste, and even considering the proportion of conventional flour with which it was combined, it meant that a new agricultural industry could be created on the back of a grass that needs no more water or fertility than our climate and soils provide naturally. A plant domesticated and acclimatised for the land – why had we spent 220 years refusing to eat what the First Australians ate? Spleen or ignorance?

In the future, millionaires are going to be made by growing and merchandising murnong and kangaroo grass, but I hope some of them are Aboriginal. Mick Dodson assures me that Monsanto makes it impossible for Indigenous people to take advantage of the intellectual property invested in their foods, but the tiny second-hand hatman of my soul believes that maybe Australians are ready to acknowledge the whole history of their country. After all, it can't be as hard to achieve as Richmond winning a premiership. The local South Coast Aboriginal food communities plan to harvest *Themeda* and market flour under their own brand.

Please, God, let Australia remember who domesticated this grain and invented bread 50,000 years before anyone else on the earth. We won't get many better chances to come together in friendship.

But remember that you can't eat our food if you can't swallow our history.

THYLACINE

I n the Australian bush at night, you could find a lost sixpence
or the feldspar in a piece of quartz; you could find the buckle
from a dog's collar or a sooty owl in a tree. But you'd never find
a pound note or an ant, and you'd never find an old sepia photograph, or why things are the way they are, although men will look
for it there, some of them all of their lives.

And so Douglas was looking again, even though he'd told his
brother he was going to check on the chooks. That cold winter
luminescence shone with such a fierce white light. Ah, it's a cold
star – a cold star bearing the steely light of a cold moon, bearing
that light without blinking, allowing it to reveal old sixpences and
feldspar, dog's buckles and sooty owls, but very little else. More
than enough light for some things, but not enough for vision.
Old iron shines like new milled steel, a shovel blade glints sharp
from the work in gravelly soil, trees shimmer like chandeliers, the
dam like a disc of stamped plate. All these old things gleam anew.
The barbed wire's rusty knots glisten with frost, spider's webs are
jewelled like the most precious things hung from the pale necks
of the world's most desirable women.

Douglas checked the chooks and they stared back at him.

Stupid chooks. He closed his fingers around the neck of a hen, and it blinked one eye but didn't move.

He checked the wire where he'd made the repair; it was still intact. Six chooks they'd lost, and not a murmur. No feathers. No wild cackles. No fox dashing about in panic and blood lust. Just a chook off the roost and a neat hole in the wire. Douglas didn't know this animal. Clarrie said a dingo or a native cat, but Douglas knew he didn't believe it himself. Clarrie knew the bush better than that, but he was the sort of bloke who always needed to propose a solution even if he knew it was wrong; anything to fill a gap.

When they'd found the human skulls, Clarrie had said it was just old-timers caught in a fire, even though he must have seen the strangeness of the sockets. Old Pearson had died out in the bush, killed by a tree that slipped back off its stump and drove his leg into the ground. Pinned him there. The bull ants stripped him clean. Clarrie had seen Pearson's skull and must have seen the difference in these others, but he just rolled them away with his boot and said it must have been two old-timers. Clarrie was like that.

Douglas saw the stones but didn't bother to tell Clarrie; he'd only argue back. So he'd returned later and picked them up and seen how the long one matched the hollow in the flat one. Douglas placed them in the crook of a tree near where the skulls had been found. Where he could put his hands on them again.

The two brothers got on alright. They could put in a row of fence posts in a day and say no more than was needed to accomplish the task – and to put in a row of stringybark posts you don't need to say a lot. There's holes and posts and a straight line. If the posts ram tight, and the eye slips along the flat faces of each post, the job's done.

Douglas didn't need people. He sold the tickets at the local dance because it meant you could stand out on the verandah and listen to the blokes yarn and maybe add your piece about the last flood, but it was a way of meeting people without going through the bother of trying to balance a noisy china cup on a saucer and think of something to say at the same time.

And the women always made him nervous. And dancing. Dancing was plain impossible. He watched other blokes dance, blokes like him, bush workers, timber millers, cow cockies, and yet they could get around; some of them just glided about.

He watched the women's bodies like the other men, but he'd never really seen one he wanted. During national service the boys had played up a bit, and that time he'd gone up to Candelo with the cricket team he didn't come back for three days. But not anyone you'd want to marry, stay with always; and anyway, who'd have him? Short, freckly bloke on a broken-down dry ridge farm. Women round here knew where the gravel pits were.

He'd never asked Clarrie. He'd never asked Clarrie anything much. Clarrie wasn't the sort of bloke you asked anything of. He guessed that Clarrie had knocked about a bit. Those trips to Bombala to sell cows sometimes took a while, but Clarrie never seemed ... never seemed lonely or anything. Clarrie always had everything worked out. Douglas thought he'd know if anything worried his brother. When the old man had died, Douglas had watched, stunned, as tears dropped from his brother's eyes. Clarrie had wiped his face with a rag and said, 'Dad taught me everything. All I know about the bush and that. That's all,' and again he had plunged his spade into the broken clay of the grave.

They got on alright, but there were times when Douglas liked to get away. The nights at the dances, the other blokes and the music, watching the women – it was just something different. And nights like this, with the cold moonlight.

He didn't tell Clarrie, you couldn't, but he knew some poems by heart. All the schoolbooks were still on the shelf. Probably never occurred to Clarrie to throw them out. The sixth-grade reader, *Modern Short Stories* and that book of French poems that came with their lounge suite at the clearing sale.

He didn't feel like it tonight, but sometimes he'd said those poems looking over the dam and down to the river: '*Slowly, silently, now the moon / walks the night in her silver shoon . . .*' Shoon, shoon. He'd worked out that it must be shoes. Their teacher had just expected them to know, but then she was the sort of jackass who'd never seen the paws of a sleeping dog in the frosty moonlight. How many people had?

He'd worked out how to say some of the French poems, too. He'd looked in amazement at the sheet music while cleaning up after a dance one night as a folded page fell from the back of a book, with the words '*non, je ne regrette rien*'. He wondered what it meant, but he found '*alouette, gentille alouette*', and suddenly the words and the song snapped to the front of his brain and he turned back to '*non, je ne regrette rien*', and he worked out how most of the words must sound; but he'd never told Clarrie. Clarrie wasn't the sort of bloke you could.

What was that?

He didn't move. He didn't even let his heart beat any differently after its initial hesitation. He could feel the hair on his shoulders and across his neck edging upwards, but he didn't move.

There it was again. A growl like he'd never heard before. He
didn't move his head, but his eyes swivelled and saw it almost
straightaway. After all, he was a bushman, and this was his yard,
and so his eyes found the strange object in it instantly. And look
at it! What an animal!

The beast had been looking at the house but felt the man's
eyes find his own, and they looked at each other, and the
barbs of glance hooked in eye flesh. Memories and visions are
made thus.

The animal was gone in the next instant, and Douglas knew
he'd be off, but he followed him to the edge of the timber and
stopped by the fence. Douglas spoke and his voice, clear and hard
in the sharp air, chased and found the beast. '*Je vous regarde* – I saw
you, dog, or … wolf. That's what you are. I saw you, tiger dog.
Thylacine.' What a word to pitch into the moonlight.

Even as it ran, the animal heard the yelling and the strange
word that was its name, and the sound would stay. Thylacine! It
stood on the dry ridge among the shards of quartz and swung
its heavy head to look down into the valley, knowing it was safe.
Surely nothing could spirit itself through time so quickly. But a
voice could, and did again.

'I know you're up there, tiger. I saw you.'

The two knew each other. The wolf would remember the voice
and the man would never forget the beast. In this universe of beings,
these two were fused by the light of a silver moon. Both hearts beat;
the tiger on the ridge, the man in the valley.

'I saw you, tiger.'

There are some things, the man knew, that could never be
denied. A man's spirit is built thus.

But animals are as logical as men, and Douglas had stood out in the bush where he knew the tiger must pass. The feldspar shone in the shafts of moonlight, the eucalypt leaves hung like small, bright scimitars of snipped tin, and the dog was there. Douglas could feel its presence by the way his hair crept beneath his collar.

'I know you're there, dog.'

At the first word, before the muscles of the legs had flung the bones into flight, the animal's eyes had seen the other's eyes above where the voice had come out of the moonshine.

'I saw you, Thylacine. You can't deny that.'

*   *   *

Some nights, man's logic and beast's logic diverged. The man knew he'd keep seeing it, although not so close to the house again. Chickens weren't that attractive. Not to a wild animal. Foxes and chickens were built for each other, but Tasmanian tigers – well, they could take chickens or leave them, and when men were around, they left them.

But some nights, out of the bush came that quiet sound. No chase, no guns, just the sound. You looked out for things like that. You didn't get too close to snakes, you kept out of the way of eagles, and, especially, you kept out of the way of men. But this one kept on being there. You never heard it; it was always where you couldn't smell it. And then, just that noise, not growling, just the same quiet sounds. No harm came, but you avoided things like that, if you could. It was better without the moon. The man wasn't there without the moon.

*   *   *

'Hey fellas, old Jack reckons he's seen a Tasmanian tiger out by the river,' Bob Ridgeway turned his big, red face over his shoulder to yell to the other blokes.

'Bull,' said Arnold Carter. 'Old Jack's been on the white lightning again.'

Old Jack didn't like Carter, so he shut up.

'He just said so,' persisted Ridgeway. 'Didn't yer, Jack; while you was settin' traps.'

Jack didn't speak. His eyes gave an affirmative, but his shoulders looked as if hoping the head's bloody mouth would stay shut.

'Keep the cork in the kero bottle, Jack,' said Carter, who knew how to use words like the whipping end of a roll of barbed wire. Jack flinched. 'Anyone else seen a Tasmanian tiger?' Carter let the last words leer. No one spoke. Douglas shuffled the last few dance tickets, and the group began chuckling and slapping broad shoulders. Jack slipped out into the moonlight, back to his camp. No one noticed. Silly old Jack, seein' bloody tigers now. Poor old coot. Trust bloody Arnold to stick in the boot, eh!

The last Palma Waltz bleated to a close. As the hall was being packed up, Douglas cast an eye over the sheet music on the piano, but this new bloke didn't use the same stuff that the other pianist had. Whatever happened to the other fella, Douglas wondered. Some blokes just disappear. Always a bit strange, that fella. Always quiet, never quite met your eyes. Except, every now and then while he was playing, he'd look up, and you'd catch him, and wonder what he was thinking. Not about the Pride of Erin, that's for sure. Douglas wondered what *non, je ne regrette rien* had meant. Could foreign words tell you anything more about a man?

*   *   *

With the new moon, the chooks began to disappear again. Sometimes Douglas would wait for the tiger in the bush. He would
crouch beside the river until the dog high-stepped through the
shallows to hide its track. 'Hello, Thylacine. I saw you again.' But
he couldn't tramp around the bush every moonlit night pretending to track a chicken thief. Clarrie'd get sick of it.

In bed, Douglas would think of the tiger, those swift glances
they had shared.

They had gotten to know each other. Douglas could see the
dog's frustration in the glances now: 'Here's that man *again*.' It was
almost like tipping your hat. The man would greet the beast with its
name, and the beast would recognise the man, recognise the voice
long before even the instant it took to find the eyes above the voice.
The man became an annoyance, like a new-fallen log across a path,
an owl that snatches the bandicoot you've tracked all the way from
the creek. To the tiger, the man became just another night animal,
and the man knew it and revelled in that pride.

Douglas lay in bed with the moon on his face, the pillow like
a field of snow. Yes, it was as though the beast no longer thought of
him as a man, but as an animal of the night, a clever one that would
sometimes appear. Not an enemy but an equal, and, strangely,
Douglas's heart strained with a feeling like ... His throat went
tight. The animal was proud, but it was more than that. It was
almost like ...

The blast of the shotgun rattled the window pane by Douglas's
face. He sat up in bed, with that strange cry still with its hooks
at his chest. He saw Clarrie with the shotgun. Clarrie turned and
looked up at Douglas's moon-white face at the window.

'I just shot at a wild dog. It won't get far. There's enough blood over here to fill a bucket.' Clarrie came over to the window holding up a finger dipped in blood. 'Thought I'd better do somethin' to stop you trampin' around the bush every night.'

Douglas stared at the blood on Clarrie's finger and felt the hairs prickling under his pyjama shirt. The claw of the beast's cry slowly released, but now there was another sensation.

Moonlight nights were terrible after that. Douglas lay in bed, and the words of poems crept across his mind, trying to close up a wound with the soft stitches of the sounds and rhythms. If, in the eleven books the brothers owned, he'd found '*Tyger! Tyger! burning bright,*' he would have read it aloud and hoped that the words would heal.

But he didn't know those words, and his mind sought for words that it didn't, couldn't, know. If they'd had the seventh-grade reader, he would have found it in there, but he didn't get to reach seventh grade. He was just a bushman.

THE IMPERIAL MIND

I t is a common vanity among humans that our ascent is an exponential trajectory applauded by God. Abrahamic religions encourage us to believe that God has never seen anything as beautiful, dutiful and intelligent as we. These religions also insist that as the devout are closest to God's hem, all others need assistance to reach that plane. The imperialist mindset, so linked with religion, suggests that realising the true destiny of humans involves reaching a certain level of social and economic, and so spiritual, development.

The magnificent vanity to assume that a god had chosen you to rule over all others. Of course, if you create that god yourself, he is likely to approve of you or face the sack. Or at least a reformation.

The planet, however, has a history of blind cul-de-sacs. The dinosaur, the dodo, the Phoenician, the Roman, the Nazi – well, not sure about the dodo and the dinosaur, but the others thought they were chosen, that their magnificence had been sanctioned by a higher force.

Hierarchies of privilege were entrenched as standard social practice during the long period of colonial hubris. Kings and priests were appointed as a means of protecting the privileges of rank, property and religion. The kings grew ambitious and the priests saw advantages in courting that ambition. Eventually, this led to kings fighting kings to extend their influence and increase their access to the riches of the world. China and certain countries in Europe fought countless wars against their neighbours to maintain or advance their position in the world hierarchy. Whole armies and entire populations were butchered, cities were sacked and peoples enslaved so that the greed and bloodlust of kings and emperors could be sated, and the flocks and coffers of the priests burgeon.

When sailing vessels were constructed of a size and stability to endure ocean crossings, the kings were quick to see further opportunities to satisfy their greed, while the priests saw opportunities to spread the influence of their creeds.

The Chinese were interested in trade, and ventured across the Pacific in search of new and exotic goods. Their communications with the new worlds were often benign, and mutually profitable in both a commercial and a social sense. The Europeans, on the other hand, sought conquest. In 1493, Pope Alexander VI introduced a papal bull, the Doctrine of Discovery, that declared when Christians discovered a new land they had the responsibility to take the land away from those they judged as heathens – that is, those with a different god. If the people resisted, they had the right to take the land by force.

For Christians, this application of theft and violence required some sophistry so that it could be squared with the Ten Commandments. The logic went that murder and dispossession could be labelled 'just wars' and applied for the benefit of the murdered and dispossessed.

According to Robert J. Miller in *Discovering Indigenous Lands,* the Spanish priest Franciscus de Victoria argued that the fact that 'Indigenous peoples were bound by European definitions of the natural law rights of the Spanish' was 'an ample excuse to dominate, defraud and then engage in "just wars" against any native nations that dared to stop the Spanish from doing whatever they wished'. The sham of natural law meant Spain's rights were seen as 'naturally' superior to native rights, based solely on the papal belief in the superiority of their conception of god.

Robert A. Williams Jnr described this assumption in his book *The American Indian in Western Legal Thought:*

> The West has sought to impose its vision of truth on non-Western people since the Middle Ages ... sustained by a central idea: the West's religion, civilisation and knowledge are superior to the religions, civilisations and knowledge of non-Western peoples. This superiority in turn is the redemptive source of the West's presumed mandate to impose its vision of truth on non-Western peoples.

This passage was never more vivid in my mind than when I visited the Museum of Anthropology in Vancouver some years ago. I stepped through the door and stared up at a two-storey façade of a First Nation house, one of the most beautiful pieces of wooden art and architecture I have ever seen. I studied the story depicted on the columns and slumped onto a seat, depressed by the idea that anyone could declare the builders of this structure 'savage'.

The story told of the world being supported on the back of a turtle, and that turtle being supported by another turtle, and that second turtle being supported by a third, and so on to infinity – had anyone seen the turtle? No, they had imagined the turtle, just as

Christians imagine haloes, harp-playing angels and God himself. To imagine a god and then proceed to the conclusion that yours is the only one is a staggering feat of illogic that bedevils the world to this day. Much violence can be attributed to the hubris of those who cling to the sacred garment of their imagined god.

To question the European presumption of an architectural hierarchy, that the built environment defines civilisation, is simply to highlight the West's arrogance, its refusal to see excellence in the work of the peoples of the lands they plundered. In fact, we must resist glorifying the edifice and making the hallmarks of success sustainability and longevity. Over aeons Australian Aboriginal people adopted the lore from one generation to the next, not without refinements and adaptation, but without moving away from the central ethic that insisted all should receive equal access to housing, food, culture and education. That insistence on sharing the benefits of life may have precluded raising architectural monuments for the sake of priests and kings. Of course, that is a long bow, but our world seems never to have considered the greatness of modesty, falling into the trap of lording the edifices of the greedy few and the enslavement of the majority to erect them.

Robert J. Miller argues the root of the Doctrine of Discovery goes as far back as the fifth century AD, when

> the Roman Catholic Church and various popes began establishing the idea of a worldwide papal jurisdiction that placed responsibility on the Church to work for a universal Christian commonwealth. This papal responsibility, and especially the Crusades to recover the Holy Lands in 1096–1271, led to the idea of justified holy war by Christians against infidels to enforce the Church's vision of truth on all peoples.

Miller writes that Pope Innocent IV decreed in 1240 that the Christian had a right to dispossess indigenous peoples because of the 'papacy's divine mandate to care for the entire world ... [and] to intervene even in the secular affairs of infidels when they violated natural law. Natural law was, of course, defined by Europeans and the Church.' The Teutonic Knights at the Council of Constance in the fifteenth century argued that land could be taken from heathens with impunity.

Justified holy war and the identification of 'infidels' highlights the intellectual and spiritual vanity of the Christian, and explains how indigenous peoples on four continents and several oceans could have their cultures attacked for not believing in the same sequence of gods and angels. Christian-derived definitions also mandated the correct way to use the soil, and those who did not use it in a fashion understood by the European legal system were deemed not to have the same human and natural rights as the Christian.

The term 'terra nullius', or empty land, arose directly from the Doctrine as one arm of the justification in breaking the Ten Commandments. Lest the Christian population see through the ruse and rebel against the ruling of the clergy, in the nineteenth century the church adopted the *Peaceable Kingdom* paintings of Edward Hicks, in which the savage animals were led into the Christian light by an innocent child. The paintings were displayed in most schools, churches, homes and government buildings, and were purportedly necessary to show indigenous peoples how to live properly. Or, as was the case for most, how to die properly.

Over centuries the Doctrine was invoked to deny any challenge to the validity of those invasions, and allowed politicians and priests to picture all indigenous peoples as savages who would fall away before the force of superior intellect and belief. Thomas Jefferson's Native American negotiator felt so superior to those to whom he was supposed to dispense some land justice that he called them children.

In 1793, George Washington described this outcome as 'the Savage as the Wolf'. Washington assumed the Native American lands would fall to the United States as their inhabitants shrank away from superior beings in the same manner as the wolf avoiding contact with humans.

This conceit was first used to try to intimidate the Mongols. The whole basis of the ruse was that the Christian religion is derived by the operation of the Holy Spirit and is therefore beyond the realm of men. As a result, it is incontestable.

The imposition of the West's superiority is still alive today. It was made explicit in 2007, when the United Nations General Assembly adopted the Declaration on the Rights of Indigenous Peoples by a vote of 143 to 4. Who were the four dissenting nations? The United States, Canada, New Zealand and Australia: the colonial governments who have most to lose if rights are extended to the indigenous peoples of these lands.

All four nations used the Doctrine of Discovery as their authority to dispossess local populations, even though, in each case, the British Crown had urged a more conciliatory and caring approach. James Cook's instructions in Australia were to 'cultivate friendship and alliance' while seeking 'the consent of the natives'. These sentiments seem to have been little more than tokenistic for parliamentary liberals, as such an approach was never a firm policy on the ground.

The Declaration on the Rights of Indigenous Peoples was drafted by dozens of countries over a period of twenty years, but only four countries in the world saw it as a threat. This was a moment of shame for Western colonial societies. Self-interest plunged these four into an alliance of denial. Hand-wringing about 'closing the gap' appeared just a smokescreen to obscure Australia's real intention: to perpetuate the dispossession and justify it with the Intervention.

One of the most important tasks of the imperial colonist is to ensure that the previous occupiers of the land are expunged from memory. Colonial southern Africa politician Cecil Rhodes made it a criminal offence for anyone to refer to the city of Great Zimbabwe, built by the Shona people in the south-east of Zimbabwe in the eleventh century. It was important to construct and embed a story of the hopeless savage so that European occupation would seem a necessary part of God's design.

In Australia, where Edward Hicks's *Peaceable Kingdom* tropes were employed as part of colonial tactics, educators, politicians and clergymen were relentless in their depiction of Australian Aboriginals as helpless savages. Their efforts proved successful because the true descriptions of the Aboriginal culture and economy were completely erased from the public conscience and, amazingly, from the public record.

Much of the material about European explorers' first contact and observation of Aboriginal Australians and their culture has been excised from textbooks, so historians, scholars, educators and nation-builders have never read it. This process has continued through each generation of scholars and educators for the past 230 years. It is an epic achievement of conniving censorship: racist in intent, and deliberate and calculated in performance.

Those early scholars, and the legions who have followed, would
have read that explorer Sir George Grey, the first Englishman in
parts of Western Australia, saw many, many fields of the tuber
Dioscorea hastifolia stretching to the horizon. He was never able to
calculate the length of the fields because they were so deeply cul-
tivated that it was impossible for him to walk across them. Each
field had well-established roads and irrigation points, and substan-
tial villages where the cultivators lived.

Charles Sturt was saved from death in the very heart of Australia
by people who were cultivating, harvesting and milling grain to
make the bread that the explorer said was the lightest and sweetest
he had ever tasted. Not only does this information never appear in
an educational or historical text, it doesn't even make it onto our
cooking shows, where we drool over other countries' recipes when
we have on record several explorers who refer to Indigenous foods
as the most flavourful they had ever eaten.

Thomas Mitchell rode through nine miles of stooked grain
on what is now the New South Wales–Queensland border. The
word 'stook' should alarm anyone who claims to know Australian
history. A stook is a bundle of grain that has been harvested, gathered into sheaves and stood on end to ripen. No Australian should
leave primary school without knowing this – but in fact all of us
do. And, most of us, secondary school, and university. It is a hor-
rible manipulation of history that two and a half centuries of good
Australians have died not knowing a fact that would transform
their understanding of their country, their culture and their soil.

Isaac Batey noticed that the hillsides of Melbourne had been
terraced by the cultivation of murnong, *Microseris lanceolata*. Due
to this agricultural practice, the soil had such a light tilth that you

could run your fingers through it. Twelve months after the introduction of sheep, the murnong had been eliminated and the soil compacted into a hard, impenetrable pan, so hard that rain ran off the surface immediately and caused the first floods the local Kulin clans had ever seen. The accepted Australian history revels in the pastoral deeds of pioneers, and we all learnt that the Australian economy rode on the sheep's back. Such is the pervasive Australian silence, however, that we have never learnt that the soil was destroyed by sheep's hooves.

As Australia has an ongoing debate about the date of its national holiday, I wonder if this new intelligence will liberate us sufficiently to search for the real Australian culture.

*　　*　　*

Chefs have been excited by bush tomato, saltbush, lemon myrtle and bush raisin for a decade or more, and laud the virtues of 'bush tucker', which makes it all the more surprising that the nutritional and economic staples of grains and tubers, the bread and potatoes of Indigenous people, have been ignored. Or is it that 'bush tucker' reinforces an image of First Nation peoples as wanderers, opportunistic hunters and gatherers, people who it could be claimed did not own or make utility of the land? I believe this selective reference to the Aboriginal economy is part of the colonial process. Unfortunately, it has robbed us of important agricultural and environmental information.

The plants Aboriginal people domesticated are, of course, Australian, and have prospered within the confines of Australia's soil moisture levels. All are adapted to Australia's environment, so require little or no water, no fertiliser or pesticides. In a drying climate – and at a time when many people accept that excessive chemical use is harming the planet, and constant ploughing is releasing too much carbon into the atmosphere – these plants could be good for the environment and excellent for the economy. Surely we have to let go of the colonial propaganda about Aboriginal land practice in order to contribute more responsibly to environmental protection and our own financial welfare? Perhaps we might even admit a truer reflection of the nation's history into our schools and the national conversation.

I spent the last few days before 26 January working with Aboriginal people to celebrate our culture and then, while travelling home, listening to Australians whinge about the Change the Date campaign. My skin is so light I often hear what mainstream Australia really thinks – and it is a scary revelation. There is incomprehension, bitterness, vindictiveness, but, most importantly of all, an impoverished understanding of the national history.

This encapsulation of ignorance is preventing our full embrace of the land. If we could understand the brilliance of the Australian agricultural mind we would meet our carbon-emission reduction targets easily. The domesticated Aboriginal grains and tubers are mostly perennial, so their cultivation requires far fewer tractor hours, thus saving the soil from compaction and the air from pollution.

The ability of these plants to flourish in our climate and soils will save us billions of dollars. The yields will not always be as great as the plants we have introduced from overseas, but can be grown over greater areas and at far less expense. Why aren't we using them? Because they question our assumption of scientific superiority and the very occupation of the continent? Well, as John Howard said, get over it.

The world is in too precarious a state to allow us to hide our heads in the sand any longer. For the sake of the country and our economy, we have to embrace the nature of the continent and the knowledge of our people, gathered over aeons as old as speech. Be proud rather than angry: this is the real nature of the land we all say we love.

CHOOSING

Her shape had become indeterminate. When shopping, the cost of extra material had been offset by economies of tailoring. She was not a large woman – in fact she was quite short – but all curves had merged. It was the brightness and intelligence of the face that captured your attention after the first moment of observation. True, she'd dyed her hair the colour of a black enamel kettle, and part of the scalp could be seen through the thinning strands, but you knew she wasn't going to give up on coiffure easily.

Her board advertised three different kinds of gluten-free toasted sandwiches for those who visited the third-last café in Tasmania. The railway that ran through five acres of rainforest was her idea. She could make sandwiches and coffee and sell tickets for the tourist train at the same time. An unusual woman. Person. Palmer imagined her politely haranguing council safety inspectors with the tourism prospects of a train that utilised the old timber-mill tramway. She probably did the canteen for the footy team over winter. Led the Landcare mob replanting rainforest trees. Hosted all the historical society meetings. Hard person to deter with bluster and by-laws.

She didn't get too many calling for gluten-free, but never mind, you just picked the slices out of the freezer. He could tell the scrubwren of her wanted to meet him, bright eye to bright eye. Inquiring. In a sentence about rainfall and the coming tourist season she found out why he preferred gluten-free and then explained about the severity of her grandniece's gluten intolerance. And what a smart child she was. And how Scrubwren had introduced her to Dickens and Tolstoy and Melville and Baynton.

'Twelve?' he asked, a little alarmed.

'Oh yes, but she *devours* books, and we talk about them all. She can't get out much, you see. Can't go to school. She's quite ill so the books are her world. And we can share it, you see.' She gave him that quick, bright look, not staring, not judging, just interested. She had him tabbed as a schoolteacher or something. And she was almost right.

'Palmers?' she said, after his enquiry about his family. You could see her brain whistling with the speed of her thought. 'Palmers.' That bright look again. The slight hesitation. 'You'll need coffee,' she said suddenly, and bustled off to get it.

There was no espresso machine so he'd resigned himself to Maxwell House. He could hear the thump of the kettle, the clink of cups, and let his gaze rove the tourist posters and brochures. Old photos. Trains in rainforest glens. Sleeper cutters leaning on adzes. Bogged bullock wagons. An old football team. Sepia with age. Or race.

When she returned, the coffee had been brewed and she had two cups and a plate of sultana-and-ginger slice. He could see the shreds of ginger in it.

'Now, I'm a Faulkner, you see, and my mother was an Anderson,

and her mother was a Doran. You need to know that because you'll
be related to them as well.'

As well as what?

'Some of your family are a little reluctant to meet strangers.
Even family, see. There's been a lot of ... unpleasantness. A lot
of people want to know about the old days. For various reasons.
You'll understand when you meet them. Mrs Arnott is the person
you'll have to talk to, the oldest, you see, green house behind the
old mill, but it's Biddy Cowland, her sister, who will give you the
most information. Out by the tennis court. Seven Grange Street.'

'Thank you.'

'Not at all, but when you come back we'll have another chat.'

They drank their coffee and dabbed at crumbs of cake. He
wondered how she could be so sure he'd be back. She just wondered. Speculatively, as good scrubwrens do.

*   *   *

Garden ornaments were not his thing, but what other people did in
their gardens was none of his business. Even so, stepping through the
door in the house behind the old mill was a shock. Every flat surface
was the throne for an overdressed doll. Except for the bench, where
a fish tank quietly slimed and myopic fish peered from within the
gloom. Two walls were honeycombed with little crypts where more
dolls sat like extras in a horror film, all flaxen hair and petticoats.

It took his breath away, or at least that part he had reserved to
talk about Aborigines. His family. Palmer found himself perched
on the hard wing chair, startled out of the ability to sit back within
its embrace of velvet. Dark blue. To sit back would cause twilight
to begin at eleven in the morning.

The conversation touched briefly on the reasons for his strait crossing but got clipped of any intimacy when he caught the stare of a blonde doll. Which meant he couldn't look at two walls or the fish tank or any of the myriad occasional tables and the watchful repose of the little person throned upon it.

He was forced to look at Mrs Arnott and notice that her Kmart tracksuit had breakfast down its front. Not stains. Bits. She was smiling and bunching her lips in rhythm with a song only the dolls could dance to. She was out of it.

Her husband didn't bother to take part in either the introductions or the conversation. He was in and out of the flywire door, off to do important things. Which couldn't wait. And then he'd clap back in and let the kettle drop onto the stove, slamming like a cell door.

He hates me already, Palmer realised. I'm not working. I'm poncing around looking for family when I should be repairing a lawnmower. In a state I hate.

Finally the serious mechanic stood in the doorway with a cup of tea Palmer knew he wasn't going to be offered, and stared. Interview with Lady Gaga over. He'd seen enough mainland wannabes trawling for the bounty of island heritage. The fuckwits.

But an airline ticket is an airline ticket, Palmer thought, and I won't be able to afford it again soon. May as well be hung for a sheep as for a lamb.

'Mr Arnott, your family is Aboriginal too, isn't it?' Palmer had never planned to ask a question as bald as this, of any geriatric aunt or mechanic uncle, but he could feel he was about to be kicked out so had to get things straight.

'So they say,' Arnott said, and he turned and left. Just like that.

Slap of flywire and gone.

Palmer looked at Mrs Arnott, but she was smiling while her lips gently mumbled a tune, a rhapsody for porcelain.

He let himself out and walked the concrete path, with its edge of embedded shells, past the rubber swan, deftly disgorged from an old tractor tyre by hands fascinated by their ingenuity, and glanced into the garage. No surprise there: full of tools. But then he looked again. A poster of a boxer. On paper gone ochre. Dave Sands, Aboriginal boxer. From an era when Mr Arnott was a young man and had heroes.

Palmer slid into the hire car and swallowed with the relief of steering away.

Of course, more time would have allowed for a more relaxed exchange. Leaning on the bonnet of an old Toyota ute, say, or slipping a few quiet ones down at the local, but he didn't have the time for bush languor – he had to get on a plane the next day. And anyway, she was his aunt. He had some rights to attention. A lot of old people loved talking to lost nephews. Not these old people, it seemed.

Who was he to judge those who had chosen to be white? It happened more often than not. For those who could. And for terrific reasons. To live being the most important of them. He'd heard the stories his uncle told, and those of cousins he'd had to track down through the phonebook, about the decisions people had to make when they could no longer feed their children. Unemployed because of one single nasty inclusion on their CV.

And who was he to choose black? Was Arnott's poster of Sands a lesser allegiance? Who was blackest? Who was best and fairest?

Yes, he knew all the soiled confusion, had read the letters to the editor scoffing at the choosers, as if there had never been a war, just a transfer of title. His uncle's revelation had scared him into reading the whole sorry history, the ground opening between the black and white feet like a quaking of the earth. Of course the reality demanded adjustments, but was the only response a house of dolls and an oil rag?

He travelled over the ridge and paused halfway back to the estuary to photograph the gate of the house built by a white great-grandfather, and later the orchard, the only remaining evidence of the house of the Aboriginal side. The black Cowlands.

It wasn't as though he was ignorant or even unsympathetic, but the pains and humiliations of his parents had set his teeth grinding on the grit of his country's history. That's what he'd come for, to find the point where the families and colours intersected.

*   *   *

'Knew you'd be back today. Bart saw your car coming down the mountain. Got the bread out of the freezer already. And I made some of that cake, too. Got a tin for you to take back to Victoria, unless it's a prohibited import over there.'

This was the kind of warmth and humour Palmer had been hoping to have with his own family. The imagined conversations, chuckling over family characteristics; photos of Christmases long gone, big fish caught, the cousin who played cricket for Tasmania. He could cry for his desolation.

Turning away from the rubber swan and onto the road down the mountain, he'd bound himself in such a rigid girdle he only remembered to breathe when he found himself wobbling at the wheel. All the planning. All the country romance. All the reminiscence. All the love.

'They're a bit funny, I know, but they do get a lot of professors bossing them around about the past.'

'I'm not a professor.'

'I know, my dear, but they're the same questions, aren't they? They think people are having a go at them or trying —'

'To get something?'

'Well, that's how they think. They've had it hard, that family. Your family. And I know you're not trying to take advantage, but it's how they are, they're defensive. Anyone would be. It doesn't help you ... But you haven't told me your name?'

'Thomas.'

'Well, of course. It's a family name, isn't it? Yes, your great-grandfather's name in fact.'

He was too tired and brittle to revive hope of cheerful conversations.

'Now, Thomas, you mustn't feel too disappointed. Give them time. Come back and stay a few days. You can sleep in our cabin if you like. The train doesn't start running until nine. Then you can see all the family. In their own time. Mrs Arnott is a bit quiet, but Mrs Cowland will show you all the photos, the family tree, she'll take you out to all the spots where your family lived, I'm sure. Biddy and I play golf together, Thomas. Well, we don't actually play much golf, we do a lot of walking and looking for the ball, but we talk ... our two families have seen it all. There's so much to talk about. You'd be surprised.'

'And you haven't told me your name.'

'Of course, but you looked like you didn't care. I'm Elizabeth Garland. My great-grandfather shot your great-grandfather.'

TRUE HUNTERS

T he psychology of land use is fundamental to the understanding of any civilisation. Even more important is the nation's relationship with the native fauna. That relationship, as many philosophers have said, defines the very nature of humanity.

Our relationship with the kangaroo is as emblematic of us as the roo is of the national crest. That the kangaroo is mown down daily by road transport, tangled in farm fences and its habitat whittled away hardly impacts on the public consciousness, but should someone suggest a cull of a roo population on an army base, the nation begins an episode of shallow breathing.

The wholesale destruction of koala habitat barely rates a mention in the press, but when koalas eat out a remnant forest on an Aboriginal reserve at Framlingham the *Kirrae wurrong* are accused of mismanagement and the issue features several times on national television with never a question about why there is only one remnant of this forest type in the area.

Deer were introduced, along with foxes and pheasants, in colonial Australia because there is something altogether more gentlemanly about a ritualised British fox hunt than shooting kangaroos in an open plain. The thrill of killing a kangaroo is absent because all the iconic symbolism in the European sensibility is tied up in the rituals of fox hunting, princely falconers and gentlemanly fly fishers. To illustrate the lingering fetish with the Old World blood sports you need look no further than the logo of gentlemen's country fashion label Rodd and Gunn, which bears the image of an English quail dog. The fishing retailer The Compleat Fisherman is as British as its logo of the gentleman fly fisher decked out in plaid shooting cap and plus fours.

Australian blackfish and garfish are probably superior eating but they don't take a fly, and gentlemen use flies. The whole psychology of the Englishman is wound up in the romance and dignity of tie flying and deer stalking. So to be a gentleman in Australia you have to import the game so enmeshed in your psyche. Otherwise you're just a native-born oaf slugging around the bush in jeans and Blundstones.

The single greatest distinguishing characteristic of the non-Indigenous hunter of any land is the emphasis on sport and leisure rather than hunting for the provision of food. Even more significant is the emphasis on size, quantity and type.

The real Australian hunter is after the biggest barramundi he can get, or the biggest trout or salmon. To my taste the ocean salmon is one of the least palatable of Australian fishes, but it fights like the blazes, can be caught in the surf and often in great numbers, using massive surf rods. The same fishermen on the same beach scorn the delectable dart. They're slight little fishes, the fillets are fine, but they fry up like garfish, one of the best eating sensations in the world. The gar doesn't fight much either – he's a small fish and gives up his life with little complaint. There's almost no achievement to catching one, unless of course your aim is to provide your family with one of the finest meals the world can offer.

Indigenous fishing parties rarely took fish in roe. It was subsistence fishing, a responsibility to provide food for the community. Of course, modern refrigeration enables more fish to be caught for future meals, but only true hunters seem to count their catch by the meal; most believe they are in some kind of competition to prove their manhood.

When my family toured Australia in 1993 we provided ourselves with whiting, squid, crayfish, dart, bream, bluebone, mud crab, garfish, herring, abalone, mussels, razor clam, yabbies, bass, mackerel or zebrafish four or five nights a week. Travelling in a minute fold-up caravan, more akin to a deck chair than a home, it was our pleasure and need to provide the next meal for our table. We looked forward to ingesting the food of the country we were in, paying homage to the country and the ancestor fishers who had preceded us.

We fished with Bunjulung, Murri, Yolngu, Jaru, Nyoonga and others, eating the food of the country, learning about places and people as we went. It was our pleasure but also our introduction to country and its tempo, rules and requirements. It taught us how to behave in the country of other people.

So we were dismayed whenever we entered a new camping spot to be assailed by sport fishermen offering us a wad of poorly refrigerated flathead or whiting, fish they had wasted in their search for their real hunter selves.

My son and I would look at each other and sigh with resignation because our delight was taken from us while we ate these surplus fish. Time and again we were overwhelmed by the stench from caravan park rubbish bins where buckets of unwanted fish were dumped by trophy fishermen.

Australians haven't learnt to love their country, still being obsessed with what they can extract from it, be it unseemly riches or inflated ego. We need to encourage the True Hunter, and I meet quite a few of them but, sadly, they are a tiny minority of those who hunt.

I have a friend who goes duck shooting for thirty minutes every duck season. He hunts on two separate Sundays for fifteen minutes, during which he shoots two or three ducks. He takes them home and salivates as he laves each of them with a loving preparation before roasting them one at a time in his wood oven. It is one of the joys of his life to provide this meal for his family. In between times the ducks get fat on his bottom pasture.

One True Hunter used to catch three or four large blue yabbies from a little stream no more than ankle deep, but the location was special to her. The creek was overhung with paperbark and tree fern, and it was a place for contemplation as well as hunting. Indeed, in the True Hunter the two are wedded. This great hunter would take the yabbies home and sit by her stove while they boiled to a cherry red in the pot, cracking a chilled bottle of Abbots Lager and drinking every damn drop whether she wanted it all or not. This was her pleasure, her ritual, her religion.

An aunt requests a crayfish for her birthday each year and celebrates her age by savouring the firm, sweet flesh she remembers from her youth, and she too likes a beer or a wine, for her health you understand, and then she likes to dance, doesn't matter what the music; she's found she can dance to anything, and why not at her age.

I had the good fortune recently to fish for two days with a remote country bushman. Two days of quiet, sporadic conversation: but every bird noticed and named, every stealthy approach by an animal observed, every minute alteration in the river's behaviour analysed, the history of every abandoned cottage intimate. Slowly the pages of that country were turned and revealed, a graceful, passionate recitation of country.

It was very Aboriginal in style and intent, the direction Germaine Greer believes is inevitable for Australia's true birth into nationhood. All of us True Hunters.

That man's brother, a saw miller by trade, was the gentlest, most kindly man I have ever known. He was not Aboriginal either but he taught me so much about country, about decency and respect. He'd notice some rare bird or tiny creature and he'd sneak a look at you with a child-like smile of delight on his lips. He was deeply, passionately in love with his country. Not for Alex the aluminium Hornet Trophy with 100-horsepower motor – no, Alex liked to lie on his guts beneath a paperbark and spin out line from a hand reel. 'They can't see ya like this, can't hear ya either, they're finicky, fish.' He liked to use *toredo* as bait too, the transculent worm that grows in submerged tree limbs, and he taught me how to eat it the way he'd been shown, blackfella way.

Australians need to love their country, love their countrymen and women and love the food our country gives. We should salivate at the thought of cooking our country's fish and fowl, not slaughtering them in some kind of game show where most is best. If the colonists had followed the example of the Indigenous True Hunters, they wouldn't have drained the Sandringham swamps, and today we'd still be eating Magpie geese and Cape Barren geese

for our birthdays and Christmases. But in those days draining wet-
lands was the surest way to get a knighthood; shooting geese for dog
food or just for the fun of slaughter was seen as good, manly sport.

The Americans shot out the buffalo in a decade, destroying
one of the world's most massive migratory herds. While much of
the slaughter was to clear the land for domesticated stock and to
drive out the Native Americans, part of the motivation was male
posturing through sport: trophy hunting.

That temperament, that psychological imperative, separates
you from the country. It allows you to live there but it never allows
you to feel at home; you're always so hell bent on changing the landscape, forcing it to do your bidding. It prevents Australians feeling
love of country because we never approach it without a weapon.

You might think this has nothing to do with history, that fish
and fowl mean nothing in terms of nationhood, but our reaction to
our country has a mighty impact on our use of country: the introduction of animals and plants to salve nostalgia drastically affected
the value of agriculture, the careless, indeed prideful removal of
habitat, eliminating resources that would be of great utility and
inspiration to us in the future.

Eating is a fundamental determinant of history. When the
squatters arrived at the Colac lakes they found the land teeming
with pigeons, ducks, emu and bustards, while the kangaroos were
sighted in countless numbers. So numerous were the ducks that if,
after a two-hour absence, the shooter did not return with twelve
to fifteen fine black mallards, they thought the supplies must be
falling off to an alarming extent.

Today some of these same lakes are rendered completely sterile
by dairy effluent. For decades waste milk products and sewage

were pumped directly into the lakes. The fine little smelt the first Colac squatters stole from the fishing nets in 1836 have all but disappeared. What goes on in the mind of man when he sees a body of water like that and dumps his waste in it, shits in his water supply? The Colijon never did that – like all Aboriginal people, they were meticulous in the disposal of their waste. They'd never even camp right on the river bank lest they foul it.

Very few colonial reports ever refer to the beauty of the land other than the delight of the waving grasslands to their eyes. But they were destroying it. And the man in the plaid cap or the hunting hat, with all his stupidities and vanities, was one of them.

LAMENT

TEMPER DEMOCRATIC,
BIAS AUSTRALIAN

As late as 2006, the then deputy leader of the Liberal Party, Julie Bishop, supported the idea that Aboriginal children should not be taught their own culture and language because it would retard them. Her fellow ministers and advisers weighed in with the opinion that Aboriginal culture was flawed because we hadn't invented the wheel or done anything useful with the land. Some went so far as to say child abuse was one of our cultural traits.

There is nothing postcolonial about Australia. It still has a Raj mentality and a vindictive adherence to colonial myth. Our country has never really investigated the colonial legacy, preferring to express horror at the inadequacy of the Indigenous population and the need to control their destiny and band-aid the wounds. If a crisis in health and education is perceived, it is better to send in the army rather than teachers and doctors.

Taking the land from people as the spoils of religious wars, made more efficient and lethal by the creation of great ships, allowed the Europeans to extend their influence to all continents. That the Chinese visited many of those continents before the Europeans but chose to socialise and trade with the inhabitants rather than murder them and steal from them is another story and another psychology.

The European brain was so intrigued by its own superiority that it rendered every other civilisation encountered as savage. It didn't matter that the First Nations people of Vancouver built two-storey houses, that the Pueblo had advanced cities, that the Aztec and Mayan were as wealthy as any other nation on earth, that the Australians invented bread and society. Yes, society, for the world's oldest town – and oldest by many thousands of years – is found in western New South Wales. Of course, Australians refuse to visit the fount of civilisation because it questions every myth we make about ourselves.

For Christians to remain Christian and worthy of their religion, the people they kill must be asking for it, and the land they steal must be handed to them like a windfall apple. But the church had a way of helping the Christian conscience sleep at night in dreams of civilised excellence. In 1493 Pope Alexander VI decreed a papal bull called the Doctrine of Discovery. In response to the voyages of Columbus, the Pope decided the church must explain and ratify the attacks on Indigenous peoples and the theft of their lands.

The rationale went like this. If a people did not recognise the name of Jesus Christ – and you'll be surprised how many on different continents did not – it was the duty of the Christian to take their land and bring them into the light. Most of those brought into the light had that light extinguished immediately by Christian swords. Many Christians still yearn for the same solution. As do many Muslims.

The poverty of the European spirit and the devilry of its intelligence created a massively unequal world, and that inequality was blamed on indigenous peoples instead of on the nature of the European mind. In Australia that meant crushing the oldest civilisation on earth and the creators of bread, language, society and democracy.

Almost no Australians know anything about the Aboriginal civilisation because our educators, emboldened by historians, politicians and the clergy, have refused to mention it for 230 years. Think for a moment about the extent of that fraud. Imagine the excellence of the advocacy required to get our most intelligent people today to believe it. Imagine the organisation required in the publishing industry to fail to mention Aboriginal agriculture, science and diplomacy. Don't blame Pauline Hanson, don't blame Geoff Blainey and Keith Windschuttle, blame Manning Clark, Gough Whitlam and every editor of *Meanjin* and *Overland,* for they too were guilty of that omission.

What omission? Well, let's look at what the explorers reported of the Aboriginal agricultural economy and see if you can remember any priest, parent or professor alluding to it. Lieutenant Grey in his 1839 'exploration' of parts of Western Australia, so far unseen by Europeans, saw yam gardens more than five kilometres wide and extending a distance past the horizon, and because the land had been so deeply tilled he could not walk across it. Sir Thomas Mitchell, in the country that is now the Queensland–New South Wales border area, rode through 17 kilometres of stooked grain that his fellows described as like an English field of harvest.

Mitchell saw these yam fields stretching as far as he could see near Gariwerd (the Grampians). He extolled the beauty of these plains, assuming that God had made them so that he could 'discover' them, not once thinking how peculiar it was for the best soil in the country to have almost no trees. This was a managed field of harvest. George Augustus Robinson saw women stretched across those same fields of horticulture in the process of harvesting the tubers.

E.M. Curr noticed that as he brought the first vehicle into the plains south of Echuca, his cart wheels 'turned up bushels of tubers'. Once again, some of Australia's best soils were almost bereft of trees, the plains having been horticulturally altered to provide permanent harvests of tubers. Unlike Mitchell's self-indulgent congratulations, Curr was aware who had produced this productivity and later recognised it was his sheep that destroyed it.

*   *   *

James Kirby is one of the first two Europeans in the country of the Wati Wati, near Swan Hill. He passes gigantic mounds of bulrushes stacked up and steaming and wonders about the vast enterprise but never thinks about the productivity of that plant. Aboriginal people were harvesting the base of the stem as a delicious salad vegetable and making mounds of the leaves to process starch, just one more source of baking flour.

Kirby notices a man fishing on a weir his fellows have built across the river. Well, Kirby assumes with great reluctance that blacks built it, but only because he knows he is the first white man to see it. The construction of the dam includes small apertures at the bottom so that water and fish movements can be controlled. Kirby describes the operation:

> [A] black would sit near the opening and just behind him a tough stick about ten feet long was stuck in the ground with the thick end down. To the thin end of this rod was attached a line with a noose at the other end; a wooden peg was fixed under the water at the opening in the fence to which this noose was caught, and when the fish made a dart to go through the opening he was caught by the gills. His force undid the loop from the peg, and the spring of the stick threw the fish over

the head of the black, who would then in a most lazy manner reach back his hand, undo the fish, and set the loop again around the peg.

The man refuses to look at Kirby even though he knows Kirby is watching. Already the Wati Wati have decided interaction with Europeans is not to their advantage, but he seems proud of his technique. You could say his manner is insouciant.

But how does Kirby explain the operation? He writes, 'I have often heard of the indolence of the blacks and soon came to the conclusion after watching a blackfellow fish in such a lazy way, that what I had heard was perfectly true.' So Kirby renders weirs and constructions, machinery and productivity, as laziness. Wasn't he describing an operation that would fit neatly into any description of European inventiveness and industry?

Now, for reasons that are almost impossible to explain, I recently found myself at the meetings of two different universities where staff were asked to beam with excitement because their university had been ranked twenty-third (the first) and seventeenth (the second) in the world for a particular area of scholastic endeavour. The first ten horses at the Melbourne Cup win something; I think the tenth horse gets a biscuit of hay and the jockey a wallet that Uncle Alec knocked back last Christmas. And I've seen underage soccer teams where every child got a trophy. But twenty-third and seventeenth: isn't that a bit like every toddler getting a Kinder Surprise?

We seem desperate for the world to acknowledge our excellence but unable to investigate our own history. We have had 230 years of scholarship in Australia from more than twenty-five universities, but no scholar has wondered about the Aboriginal domestication of plants and the vast fields of agriculture witnessed

by the explorers, the so-called unchallengeable founts of knowledge of Australian history.

   We stab out our eyes rather than regard Aboriginal achievement
in this country. Our best citizens go to extraordinary and under-
standable lengths to protect innocent refugees from persecution,
but we still allow First Australians to have their money quarantined
for crimes that have never been tested by our courts.

   The reason for the national apathy to racial politics in this
country stems, I believe, from the national ignorance of Aboriginal
culture and economy, and that ignorance has to be laid in part at
the feet of our learning institutions. A legion of professors and
other academics at our universities decided it would be unnecessary for our golden youth to know what the explorers witnessed
of Aboriginal excellence.

   We seemed bemused when the over-ploughed soils of the
Wimmera blew about our heads in Melbourne in the sixties, seventies and eighties. Today we wring our hands because the Darling
River stops flowing in January; we wonder why we cannot get a
second yield of hybrid blue gum from the forests of Tasmania,
Western Australia and Victoria, so in apparent wrath at the vagaries
of nature we poison that weedling second crop. We have ruined the
soil but blame greenies for crop failure and unemployment rather
than poor science and the massive and soil-destroying machinery.

   But like the baker's blinkered horse, we cannot look behind,
we cannot admit that First Nations land management, finely tuned
over 120,000 years, might have the ability to clear fog from our
brains. Even today our agricultural scientists seem surprised when
the Aboriginal domesticates thrive in the soils and climate to which
they were born.

Oh, we love to talk about bush tomato, lemon myrtle and wattle seed because they fit our venal understanding of hunting and gathering, but when asked to consider the virtues of agricultural products grown on fields so wide the explorers could see neither their beginning nor their end, we become flummoxed and querulous. These crops are perennial; they were staples of Aboriginal diet and economy. The word 'staple' suggests permanence and utility, and both the latter were the sole basis for the application of terra nullius.

*   *   *

I don't mean to berate, but the hour is late. Aboriginal health and education continue to fall far below the national average, and the incarceration rate of Aboriginal Australians should be the shame of the nation instead of a prickly nuisance. Australia seems to wash its hands of this state of affairs, never seeming to wonder how dispossession and our fabricated pre-colonial and postcolonial histories works on the psyche of Aboriginal and non-Aboriginal people alike.

If we are to make a nation rather than a mere economy, we have to absorb the history. Aboriginal people don't need to worry about how we got here, because archaeology seems to be proving our own belief that we've always been here. The issue is how the rest of the population got here ... and who to thank.

Australia is a drying continent. World and national inaction on the human contribution to climate change is leading to a situation where we will soon be growing mangoes in Canberra. Aboriginal domesticates do not require any more moisture than the Australian climate provides. These plants are an environmental boon to the nation, apart from the fact that, as they are all perennial, with the large root masses of plants adapted to dry conditions, they sequester carbon. If we dedicated only 5 per cent of our current agricultural lands to these plants, we would go a long way towards meeting our carbon-emission reduction targets.

The biggest opportunity Australia has is the chance to begin a conversation with Aboriginal Australia about the real politics of our history. Forget the gnashing of teeth and the gushes of tears over the current state of affairs, let's get down to tin tacks. We can and will provide employment for remote Aboriginal communities, we can and will provide health and education professionals in these communities, we can and will enjoy the improvement in national wellbeing, and we will do it as a public because the political system is failing us.

We know politicians will refuse to consider anything that challenges their control. Parliamentary vision is dead. When any prime minister wrings their hands and sheds tears of remorse, you know at the first drop of moisture that they intend to do nothing. Aboriginal and Torres Strait Islander people meet at Uluru and despite the diversity of opinion, the frustration, the old human enmities, they thrash out a statement so modest, so considerate of reality that many Indigenous people are appalled that something so vague and general can be the product of such long consideration. And the prime minister of the time, Malcolm Turnbull, dismisses it as too ambitious.

Australians will have to do the hard yards themselves. A parliament that includes lawyers can draft legislation; they just can't imagine what has to be drafted. We might allow the politicians to think our plan is their idea – sometimes it's the only way to make them concentrate – but we have to formulate that idea, and it has to be done after long consultation with Aboriginal Australia. Real talk, equal talk, not reconciliation or a Recognise or Close the Gap formulated on the assumption of inadequacy, but a true conversation about what has been lost and what gained, and how that has forged the schizophrenic national psychology.

We have to read Sturt, Mitchell, Warburton, Giles and Gregory, and we have to try to quell the triumphal urge while we read; we have to try to read beyond the daring and hardship of the explorers and the vast riches they discovered; we have to read for the cultural economy of Aboriginal Australia that they witnessed and described.

We also have to restore the sections in Lieutenant Grey's journal where he speaks about Aboriginal housing, irrigation, agriculture and road-making, because when the journal was edited for publication those were the only items left out. Maybe that's the job of a university that doesn't want to be satisfied with a Kinder Surprise for being twenty-third in the world at something; maybe there's a university that wants to investigate the roots of the oldest civilisation on earth, the civilisation that invented bread, society, language and the ability to live as 350 neighbouring nations without land war – not without rancour, for that is the human condition, but without a lust for power, without religious war, without slaves, without poverty, but with a profound sense of responsibility for the health of Mother Earth for more than 100,000 years.

This is not a noble savage sentiment, it is the iron-clad rigour gained from reading the true history of the country. I think Australia is capable of this rigour. I think we must absorb the pain and weariness such rigour will demand of us.

Temper democratic, bias Australian.

LAMENT FOR THREE HANDS

for the last three hands at Big Yengo

We were both married to other people. Now we're not. She's got this kid. Looks at me as if I'm not his father. True. I'm not. Can't be helped. That's how it is.

She looks at me as if I'm not her husband. Correct. But that's not my fault either. We're living together. The way it works out. She looks about the new joint as if she's lived in better places.

She doesn't say anything. Looks after the place: keeps it clean, cooks, keeps the kid quiet. Brings it in to bed with her though, when it cries.

Not a bad kid. Not saying that. Not at all. But my guts are twisted up with its sorrow. And hers. And I've already got my own. None of us would have chosen this. None of us.

But that's how it is. So I'm sitting out the front frigging around with a stick, just stripping the bark off it. Nothing particular in mind. Looking out over the valley. Thinking.

It's a million-dollar view. Grassy flats beside the winding river, forest climbing the mountain behind it. Beautiful. Anyone would say so, but we're not from here. The previous owner's pet bird is dancing around in front of me. *Chitter, chitter, chitter, sweet, sweet, sweet.* Yes, yes, I know, we're strangers. No, I have no idea where your mates are. Although I could guess. But how's that going to help?

Meat and potatoes cooking. Smells alright. Nothing wrong with her cooking. And she brought me a drink. Handed it to me. Said nothing. But looked at me as if to say, I'm trying. We all are. Even the kid. Washed the potatoes. Didn't have to be asked. Put 'em in the oven. Helped his mother do the meat. He's having a go. No doubt about it. Just can't bring himself to look at me. Much. Better off without the much.

She's younger than my first wife. Happens a lot, I suppose. And there's no doubt that she's prettier. Well, the old girl was getting on fifty-five. The breasts, you know what I mean. Not cheeky, not pouting, not thumbing their noses at you like this one's. And the old girl's bum, you know what I mean. But I'd have her back tomorrow. Except it can't be.

Oh, I've fucked this one. Too right, and even though her heart wasn't in it, it was good. You know what I mean, a young woman's body. The hardness, the springiness of the waist, those firm little tits nudging at you, like possums giving cheek. Oh, I enjoyed it alright. And I'm not ashamed. It's how it is. Now.

But, yes, I'd take the old girl back, slack belly and droopy tits notwithstanding. She used to run her hands all over me, if she felt like it. She'd even take a grip of me, take things into her own hands, so to speak. And when we were into it her hands would roam over my back and neck … but this one, her hands are still. Just waiting. For it to be over.

Chitter, chitter, chitter, sweet, sweet, sweet. Yes, yes, I know.

Grown man crying. Yes, he's a sorry stage of proceedings indeed.

A quarkel-doo, kool parkle-dark, koo-dool poo-keep. Bloody friar bird, clown prince with a buckled nose. Of course I know all their names, know their stories too – well, we're country people after all. Still no reason to laugh at me.

Those birds should be our comfort, our balm, we should be reassured to hear them, but all they're saying is, you're not from here, you're not from here, I want the lady who fed me crumbs.

Well, it's not my fault, I can tell you, living in someone else's place. Sleeping in their bed, cooking in their oven. Not our bloody fault. None of us.

We sit together and eat, but she serves me first, gives me the best bits, the leg and breast; the kid gets the wings and ribcage. Still nice what they have, but she's making sure she does it right. To please me. I appreciate that. I really do. A tiny comfort.

Neither she nor the kid says anything, don't meet my eye. I finish my meal, wipe my hands. Look at them.

'Alright, I know what you're thinking, I know you wouldn't have chosen this. Me. But that's how it is, we're stuck with each other and we'll have to make the best of it. This,' and I indicated the room where we sat, 'this is as good as I can do. I wish we could be in the old place, but ... things have changed. You know, you – look, none of us wanted this but ... but I'm telling you this is the best I can do for us. What I'm saying is we'll have to make the best of it. If I could find us a better place I would, but look ... I mean, we've got the river, the hills, it's not bad. Not as good as the last place but ... I think we should make the best of it.'

The boy has his head down, pretending to be engrossed in getting meat off the wing. At least he is eating again.

I stare at her and she looks at me askance. I indicate the boy with a jut of my chin. Her eyes understand.

'I think we should see if we can … just make the best of it … try and make it a home, make it ours.' I look around the place again, see how stark it is. 'Don't think I'm proud this is the best I can do. I'm not. And don't think I'm not feeling … just … what I'm saying is, what alternative is there?'

They say nothing. They aren't rude or anything, they just can't get their spirits up. And I can't blame them.

But that's what I'll do, tomorrow I'll bring home something really nice to eat. There's enough potatoes and salad vegetables in the previous tenant's garden. They'd obviously put a lot of work in. Sorry they're not here to see the fruits of their labour. I can see they loved their fruit and veggies. I won't change anything, the way they've organised it. Wonder how long they were here.

When I get up next morning, nothing much has changed. But she does look at me – doesn't smile, but it is like, Sorry, I can't help it. I know that. But I am grateful for that look. Small mercies.

Bugger it. That look lifts my heart enough just enough to think, Bugger it, I'll go fishing.

There is a corner where the river does a big turn hard up against a dark, flat wall of rock. Maidenhair ferns cascade off the terraces where the rock is flawed and fissured. Nice spot for a bit of a quiet fish.

I wish … now, now, what did I tell myself about thinking like that. It's over and she's not coming back. This is now, and besides, there's fish.

These scrub worms are just fantastic bait. Look, he's picked it up, feeling it, ready, ready, careful. There he goes, off like a shot, let him go a bit, let him swallow it, hold, hold, hold, steady, *got him,* big bastard ... Oh, this will do it, surely, bring a smile ... But really, maybe even the biggest perch I've ever caught may not be enough. Still, we'll see.

I look at the fish in my hands. A grand animal. The undershot jaw giving it the look of a real hunter, a sharp shooter of the pool.

I put him in the basket and throw another bait in, knowing I probably won't get another fish out of this hole. Lean back against the rock feeling the cool shade on my face. Doze a bit. Think about her. Getting home. Trying to make it up to her. And the boy. Not his fault.

I wake up and a platypus is drifting in the middle of the pool. Looking at me. Well, in my direction, anyway. Short-sighted little bastard. Something else to tell them about.

And when I get back, the oven is ready and she has the bar-beque prepared for the fish. Her confidence pleases me. I try to catch her eye. Not biting.

It is a terrific meal. She gets the coals just right. The skin of the perch blisters away from the perfectly white, juicy flesh. It heart-ens me. If we keep doing this for a while, we'll ... you know, just kept going ...

'I know,' I say as she is cleaning up after dinner, 'let's paint the house. Together. Brighten it up a bit.'

They look at me. Waiting.

'It'll be good, make it ours.'

They just look at me. Waiting.

So I get up and grind some pigment and mix it with water. 'Here,' I say to the boy, 'come on, you first. Put your hand like this.'

Dutifully, and I'll have to say it, sorrowfully, he puts his hand against the wall and I scoop some ochre yellow, put a portion in my mouth and stencil around his hand.

'See, look at that,' I say, 'that's fantastic.' This cheeriness is killing me. Specially with a mouthful of ochre.

I put my own hand against the wall and spray it with colour.

'Now you,' I say, as brightly as I can manage, and try to smile at her, but even to me it feels like the creak of a girth strap.

She puts her hand against the wall but averts her face, looking neither at me nor at her hand.

I hold her wrist as I spray the ochre. When I come to the gap between the first and little fingers I think I feel a sort of spasm in her arm, but I hold it and complete the job. Keep hanging on to her hand, holding it there to make a good impression. Such a young hand to have two missing fingers. For the two dead husbands lost in the war.

I rinsed my mouth but never let go of her wrist.

'There,' I said, '*chez nous.*'

ANDREW BOLT'S DISAPPOINTMENT

My friends, take a breath, lean across the table and assume the tone of Richard Dawkins explaining dinosaurs to intelligently designed Christians.

The people here believe that in my promotion of Aboriginal achievement I'm simply being loyal to family or wanting to take a belligerent stance on our country's identity and history. Houses, crops, agriculture, *sewing!* Their frustration is benign, their love for me is no less, but they think I've gone too far this time. Writers are supposed to be mad, and they are to be coddled for it like raving aunts. They are supposed to be heretical, but they are not supposed to defy everything we were taught about Aborigines. They must not be encouraged to refute the national story.

We each sit there, against the backs of our chairs, a little disappointed with the other's company. Perhaps this is too strong. Disconcerted might be the better word. We are looking at each other across a gulf of incomprehension. We are concerned that one of us is a liar and the other a denier.

I am one of Andrew Bolt's disappointments. I didn't know I had offended him until a friend sent me a copy of the column in which I was pilloried by Bolt for deciding to be black. People expected me to be outraged, but my inclination was to wish I could have a yarn with Bolt over a beer. Except he doesn't drink beer, I was told, just good red wine. Sad, the impasse we have just because histamines play havoc with my arthritis.

I can see Bolt's point, and the frustration of many Australians when pale people identify with an Aboriginal heritage. The people he attacked for this crime, however, had an unfortunate thing in common: their credentials were impeccable. Any good reporter could pick up the phone and talk to their mothers about their Aboriginality until the chooks went to roost.

If I had been part of the group who took Bolt to court for impugning their heritage, he would have had a field day. My mother's dead, and even if she had been alive she knew precious little about her family background. He would have found that my cousin had discovered the woman we *thought* was our Aboriginal ancestor was, in fact, born in England.

Having got that far, I hope he would have delved deeper and found that both my mother's and father's families had an Aboriginal connection. I was amazed to find that the families knew each other in Tasmania years before my father met my mother at a Melbourne Baptist church.

But was it an accident? The two families lived close to each other in Melbourne, in the same street in Tassie, and had Aboriginal neighbours in both places. Aborigines signed as witnesses to their weddings, and various members of the families went back and forth across Bass Strait to marry into the other family, including some first cousins.

I'm sure Bolt would find this fascinating. It mirrors the turbulence of postcolonial Australia and explains why so many Australian families have a black connection. Why should I deny them? I would plead. They fascinate me. The very nature of their survival is heroism in a cardigan. My great-grandfather died two streets from where I lived and I never heard anyone in my family mention his name. His mother had a traditional Aboriginal name. Aren't you intrigued by that, Andrew?

I'm not saying people whispered ancient secrets in my ear or passed on sacred knowledge; what I was told amounts to a bald analysis of Australian history and society, and the injunction to watch and listen to the land, to respect the fact that we do not command the earth. I'd like to explain to Bolt that my mother told me the same thing, and I'm not sure if that is Aboriginal thought or just her general modest decency.

My insight into Aboriginal Australia is as abbreviated as my heritage has allowed. It is as if I have been led at night to a hill overlooking country I have never seen. I am blindfolded, but at dawn the cloth is removed and I am asked to open my eyes for one second – any longer and I will be killed – and then asked to describe that country.

An impression is what you would get in that second. Detail? Very little. You would be left with a feeling of the country's nature and for the rest of your life you would be searching the span of a second's memory. An impression: a shallow base from which to lecture others; a humble heritage. Humility was always valued in our family, beyond wealth or influence, and you don't shake those legacies easily.

I had to learn my Aboriginal history and I had to learn Aboriginal etiquette by making mistakes. It has not been a painless journey, filled with the excitement of acceptance and inculcation into the mysteries of a secret society.

I reckon Bolt and I would have a terrific yarn. He came from Holland as a child and was an outsider too. I reckon I'd be fascinated by his childhood, how he coped as an alien. But I'd be impatient to tell him how I was perplexed by my father's mild acceptance of my discoveries. I'm sure Bolt would want the same question answered that I do: why had no one but a rogue uncle spoken of this before?

Obviously someone, or several people, had been covering tracks, but my father's affirming nod to me after I'd spoken about our Aboriginality on ABC Radio hit me for six. I'd left him listening to the radio in my Volkswagen as Terry Lane and I did the live-to-air. Terry had a way of getting guests to confide. That's journalism, Andrew!

I walked down the old ABC stairs expecting to have the best blue with my father since he saw me on the news during the Vietnam moratoriums. But no – just the mild nod, and after that we were closer than we'd ever been. I treasure a photo from that era in which he's nursing my son, with my dog asleep on his feet. He's doing the accounts for *Australian Short Story*, a magazine venture he could never imagine would succeed. But he did lend me $10,000 to prop it up.

He only told me one story, and I've written it word for word in my novel *Earth*. It's almost the only thing we know of that past. After uncovering the lattice of our Tasmanian days I have a few more questions to ask him. Like, how much did you know, Dad? Perhaps you and me and Andrew could sit together: me with my Boag's, Andrew with his superior red, and you with your Lan-Choo because you and Mum were still saving the labels for the full dinner set.

Dad's gone, but I could talk to Bolt easily and without the least rancour because I think it's reasonable for Australia to know if people of pale skin identifying as Aboriginal are fair dinkum. No one likes an imposter. Of course, we should extend the same rigour to the Irish, Jews and Christians.

What I'd like to say to Bolty – because surely we'd be on nickname terms by then – Bolty, I'd say, why didn't you ring their mothers? Are you crook on them because they identify as Aboriginal or because they're successful Aboriginals?

Australia could be confident in leaving the matter of identity to the Aboriginal community, because it is far more rigorous in its assessment, and conducts it simply by utilising two quaint scientific tools: genealogy and the telephone.

*   *   *

Many Australians are curious about Aborigines; some, like Andrew Bolt, are alarmed, and some with solid Christo-socialist credentials get agitated at my kitchen table and lean their arms upon it and implore, at a more intimate, more insistent distance: houses, crops, agriculture, *sewing?* I've gone too far; I've exaggerated in my desire to defend the race. They understand defending the beleaguered – many do it on a professional basis – but they like to think that, true to their professions of law, welfare or education, they never depart from the realm of fact.

Houses, crops, agriculture, *sewing?* They've read their explorers, they claim: Mitchell, Sturt, Giles, Eyre and Grey. They lean in closer to urge the wayward student-defendant to reconsider. These are my friends – close enough that we know each other's families – and they have a genuine desire that I not perjure myself.

I argue that they have *not* read Mitchell, Sturt, Giles, Eyre and Grey; they have read *about* them. They've read what other Australians found fascinating about their discoveries, and it wasn't anything about the Aboriginal people. If those explorers weren't looking for inland waters and vast pastures, they were looking for gold and a line for roads and telegraph lines; they were not looking for an Aboriginal civilisation.

The story that most gets up the noses of my friends is of the crops on the Warburton River, the permanent houses, the happiness, the prosperity. Surely if this existed we would know about it, they declare – we studied the birth of Australia at university. Double majors in history, two degrees!

I had been hoping they would be delighted by the information, but it offends or embarrasses them that they have never heard it. This is neither their fault nor the fault of any single Australian. It is how we've grown up. We were indoctrinated with a certain view of history, believed by our parents and buttressed by our education. This is what I believed until 1981.

Older Aboriginal people listened keenly to my family story and assisted with connections where they could, but as the years went by they became frustrated with my ignorance, my acceptance of the Australian history we are taught to believe. With controlled impatience they explained what had happened to their families; they pointed to events on my own path where the history of Australia had shattered my family, shamed them, made them 'forget' there was ever a black aunty.

I listened in disbelief, protective of the education of which I was so proud. My cousins, sister and I had graduated from university, though we came from a family where secondary education was virtually unknown. Our grandmother revelled in our success and insisted that we treasure knowledge. We loved her, and because we were warmed by her pride we decided to find out where she came from.

I made notes and listened as patiently as I could to the Elders, but was astounded that fellow Australians could have such conflicting views of the past. I slunk off to libraries, hoping no cousin would find me checking on their mother's story. My cheeks flushed crimson as I turned page after page of the histories, police records, genealogies, settlers' diaries, explorers' journals. I'd been sold a pup by the best university in the land, not just in the history classes but in education, economics, geography and science.

The history we accepted with such equanimity is unbelievable after rudimentary examination. The story with which I try to inspire my friends is from Charles Sturt's journal of his desert expedition beginning in 1844. His second-in-command is dead, the doctor is critically ill with scurvy, and Sturt is almost blind from the same disease. Their horses can barely walk. Sturt climbs a dune and is hailed by 400 Aborigines. He is startled to find happy, healthy humans in a terrain that has claimed the lives of many white explorers and reduced his party to a tottering, vulnerable rabble.

Sturt comments on a courageous and generous act: the people have never seen a horse, but after they have sated the thirst of the stumbling explorers they turn to the strange beasts and reach out the coolamons so their fellow creatures may drink. The explorers, with teeth loose and gums inflamed from scurvy, are invited to dine on roast duck and cakes baked from the grains the Aborigines have been harvesting. In the desert! Then they are offered their choice of three new houses in the village. Houses, crops, agriculture, *baking?*

We can accept that the world is round and that smoking causes lung cancer, but we cannot seem to accept as true or pertinent what the explorers witnessed of Aboriginal society and economy. European science has produced marvels, and its foundation principle is curiosity. Why are we not curious that Aboriginal people could cultivate crops in the desert? Why do we pay no attention to the dams and irrigation techniques employed? When our farmers are so threatened by droughts, salinity, erosion and crop diseases, why do we not investigate the crops and farming techniques developed over thousands of years to accommodate the challenging characteristics of this continent?

Some have speculated that many colonists were so outraged by Aboriginal customs and the absence of Christian practice that they felt compelled to reject everything of Aboriginal provenance. And that unease has survived until the present day. Our understanding of quantum physics and medical science is unrecognisable to the knowledge we professed 200 years ago, and yet we continue to scoff at the prospect of an Aboriginal *civilisation*.

What about the unconscious? Could it be that in a Christian democratic country, the one possible justification for taking the land from the Indigenous population was that they were unworthy of its possession? Some colonists thought that positioning Aborigines in Australia was one of God's rare mistakes.

How many charities in Australia support indigenous populations in Africa? How benign do we feel when we buy an Oxfam goat for the benighted of other countries? How niggardly are we in the provision of aid to the race we have dispossessed? At home we don't buy goats – we send in the army.

*   *   *

I didn't plan to write history. I'm a storyteller. I thought that literature, while not much use to a practical world, was the best I could do to honour my grandmothers' and grandfathers' legacies. But then, in telling stories, I discovered *their* hidden stories, and as they were already dead I had to ask other Aboriginal people. The rest is history.

There are a dozen or so Australian scholars upon whose work I rely, and I dread to think what our country might have become without their courage. These people have withstood disdain and ridicule for their opinions, for their seemingly wilful misrepresentation of the country's soul. I'm a fiction writer, so I'm expected to be deranged, but the academics must have felt the isolation on the nation's self-convinced campuses.

One young scholar complained to me in 2011 that he had been warned not to quote the work of the heretic Bill Gammage. Gammage had recently released a book, *The Biggest Estate,* and my dream is that every Australian reads it. (After reading my book *Dark Emu*, of course!)

I think of Gammage sitting at a lonely university café table quietly reviewing his work. He spent a lot of time in estate, anticipating the scorn of fellow academics and preparing his responses. No doubt some of his friends have leaned across tables, urging him to reconsider his heresy: houses, seeds, sewing, *sowing?*

Another landmark scholar has become so disaffected that he has removed himself from the campus entirely and studies alone. His books are now published in plain covers in London. What a shame to let the Old Dart do our controversial publishing and thinking on our behalf.

I love my country. I am relieved to live in a place where we can go down the street to get milk and not fear getting shot at. And yet

I am surprised that in a country of such gifts and intelligence, we have edited our national history so that our children will never question our right to the soil and will learn to express surprise at the ingratitude of those we dispossessed. They will be astounded, confused and belligerent at the very mention of Aboriginal achievement. Houses, agriculture, sewing, baking!

Justice holds up the scales of judgement and wears a blindfold so that no partiality is allowed. In Australia we prefer our children to dispense with the scales of justice and make do with the blindfold. The rest of the world can see the donkey ears above our blinkers: it is only here we believe they are invisible.

BIG YENGO

He's got a temper on him. You have to watch your Ps and Qs. Sometimes the entire alphabet. But he can cook, sing, play the guitar, set up a great camp. Bastard.

He patronised me a bit. Never had previous opportunities, so this was his time to be in charge.

'There's something I want to show you,' he said. I've made it sound like he was looking down his nose, but he wasn't. Just particular about what wood went on the fire, how it was stacked, where the billy sat. That's alright, I knew where he'd learnt it. From an expert. Damn near genius.

'Good,' I replied, having no idea what he thought I should see.

His job was tracking feral animals. I drove the 4WD and he ran ahead as we travelled the kilometre between each of the sand pads. Fit as a mallee bull. I was proud. He was a man in his prime; and a good one at that.

He was showing off to his father, but only a bit, just needing to convince me of his strength and capabilities. And I was convinced.

He didn't need me there, but it was an OH&S thing to have an offsider, and his footy mates were over it or in Afghanistan.

He played in Richmond, near the airforce base. Their political discussions were proscribed.

I liked that about him. No point hating people just because you disagreed. And half the flying lads knew it was a dud war. But dud wars were how they made a living, and retired early on a comfortable pension. Attractive package. If you don't get shot.

'It's over there.' He pointed towards a high ridge line just visible through the forest. 'Look down over the whole valley from up there.' He finished recording the tracks on the sand pads, checked the images on the movement-sensor cameras. He was after cats and foxes, but most of the visitors had been wombats and wallabies.

He shifted me out of the driver's seat and took over for the climb up to the distant ridge. Creek crossings, switchbacks, fallen logs across the track. It was almost dusk when we arrived.

We stood on an exposed ramp of granite. 'See them?' he said. 'The emu feet?' He pointed as he walked up the sloping granite. 'And this, where they stop, is where Baiame left the earth and went up into the sky.'

My son, telling me about Aboriginal heritage.

'They've drawn – well, not drawn, chiselled – his image across there, can you see it? Same as in the Milky Way, the Dark Emu.'

We were silent, looking at these ancient marks of passage.

'Darug mob did it.'

A third of Australia believed in Baiame as the creator, but this was his story – the Darug had shown him – and so it was his story to tell me. I was moved. Not just by Baiame's ascension from this granite tor, but that my son should find it precious, and beautiful.

We were almost silent on the way back to camp. We'd be more animated in the morning, when we discovered a goanna had swallowed my sandshoe, but now it was dark and we concentrated on the curry, which had excelled itself while sitting in the bed of warm coals. There was a smokiness to it. He'd chosen blackwood for the fire, and its smoke imparted just the right flavour.

He handed me a beer he'd stashed in his chiller, a lovely surprise. He picked up his guitar and sang all of his blues numbers, including two I'd sung to him from the day he was born.

> *Black girl, black girl,*
> *Don't lie to me*
> *Tell me where did you sleep last night?*
> *In the pines, in the pines*
> *Where the sun never shines*
> *I was shiverin' the whole night through.*

We disagreed about the lyrics, but he was insistent. He'd googled them. I'd been wrong for fifty years. Except everyone had sung this song, and the lyrics changed depending on whether the singer was incarcerated, black, white, rich or poor. But not worth arguing about.

He found two more beers as the owls began to call. I let him tell me which call belonged to which species.

He strummed away and then found his way to Woody Guthrie, to another song I'd sung to him while he was still a baby. He wasn't to know my version of the lyrics were as accurate as poor memory and deafness would allow.

> *Snow, snow, falling down*
> *Falling down all over the old town,*

Smothers the garbage dumps, smothers the tracks
Covers the footsteps of those who knocked me back.

I began to wonder about the man who would sing those songs to his babies, but before regret could become guilt, he was singing,

Keep a watch on the shoreline
There's a boat that's lost out there ...

When he was a baby, one who found it difficult to sleep, we used to take him at dusk to a sandstone ledge from where we could see the Cape Otway Lighthouse begin its watch on the shoreline. It was a habit, a ritual for our tiny family, and we knew it was imprinting itself on each of us, even the dog; too lovely for even a border collie to ignore.

Any time my wife and I see a lighthouse we still call, 'Look out, look out, there's rocks out there,' and look at each other wishing that period of our lives could have lasted forever ...

Rubbish. He was a baby who hardly slept, and we had so little money we didn't have two cups that matched. We can grieve for that time because of its innocence, but it's a trick of memory. At least now we own a complete set of cutlery ... even if our cups still don't match.

I looked at his camp things. He went for the classical. Camp oven with a dished lid so you can pile the coals on to cook bread. Old-fashioned enamelled mugs, a billy as black as the inside of a dog. Classical.

The owls called for five minutes, maybe longer, but I was asleep as soon as I drew the sleeping bag up to my neck. Happy as any man the universe had created.

*   *   *

Next day, he waves me down as I draw the ute up beside his sand pad. 'Something else you'd better see.'

It's not grudging or patronising. I can tell by now that it delights him to show me something I've never seen. Who's the big man now?

We sit on a grassy bank to take off our boots so we can wade across the stream to a low, broken plateau. He has to check his bearings and make corrections to our course until finally we are below the edge of the escarpment.

'In here,' he says, and we climb behind the boulders and up into the cave. He's looking at me, waiting to see if I can see it. The hands. Three sets of hands, one big, one with two fingers missing, one tiny. I'm broken with grief, surprised to have been so vulnerable to the ambush of story.

We're still only halfway through the day's work, but I give up the driving and he doesn't even mention the fact that I've left all the work to him. I have a pad and biro and grapple with both as the ute bucks and climbs and slews its path around the mountain.

REARRANGING
THE DEAD CAT

D ead cats are upsetting, even if they are not yours. A public corpse is likely to make children cry, old ladies cross the street, and everyone else speculate on the cat's mistake.

We never take responsibility for the cat's demise. All we were doing was playing with the cat, we say. Tying its tail to the clothesline and, oops, one too many spins and it hit its head on the gully trap and died.

The family cat hanging from the clothesline is not a good look, so we try to disguise our guilt. Let's take it down and put its head against the wall. Tell Mum and Dad it ran headlong into the bricks. No, cats don't do that, Mum and Dad would never believe it.

Let's immerse it in the toilet bowl and say it drowned. No, that won't do, Mum and Dad saw the cat swim last year in Grandpa's pool. That was our fault, too.

Let's back over it in the car. But we're not supposed to drive, are we?

I know, let's say the neighbour shot it for stealing his chickens; everyone knows cats are evil little bird-killers. But we haven't got a gun. Let's just chuck it down the creek and say it ran away of its own accord.

It's a problem, the dead cat, and Australians don't want the world to condemn us for our early mistakes. In defending ourselves we usually respond by blaming the cat or claiming that we had no idea what happened to it. Christians wouldn't kill a cat or even hurt a cow, not like those nasty Indonesians, no; it's clear the cat must have run off with the Hare Krishnas.

Most children are good, until they want something they know is forbidden. Then they lie. Either to themselves or to their parents or to their god. Or to all three. And then, because the cat didn't *really* die, they can get on with being good children.

We all want to be good children. We want to be proud of our home and deserving of its love and warmth. The cat is our only problem. We glare at the mat where the cat used to sit and mythologise its disappearance. We're good at that. We're storytellers.

Tim Winton is one of the best. He wrote the magnificent *Dirt Music, Shallows* and *The Riders,* but he also wrote the book about the Pickles' cat, *Cloudstreet.*

Australia loves Winton because he taught us how to love ourselves, to recognise our humanity and our generosity ... and how to hide our great lie.

When *Cloudstreet* came out I was astounded to find a black ghost who encouraged Sam Pickles to the view that he belonged to the land. I waited to see if any reviewers would challenge this benign view of the grand Australian larceny. Silence.

A good example of this near-sightedness on *Cloudstreet's* relationship with colonial history is a 2005 article by Robert Dixon in the journal *Westerly*: it comments on the black figures in the text, but in the length of its ten pages never considers that Winton might have fudged the past, or at least not presented it in its true complexity.

Eventually I received a copy of a review that Kathleen Mary Fallon had failed, after many attempts, to have published in Australia. Fallon was outraged that the most respected Australian reviewers had chosen to see *Cloudstreet* as our fundamental reconciliation novel.

In her unpublished review, Fallon points out that all of the novel's black characters are dead. She notes:

> *Cloudstreet* doesn't want to do the hard work of struggling with 'black' Australia to find a shared history; it slumps back into trite 'spiritual' insights [such as] 'there's no them, only us', rejuvenated Christianity and a feel-good, heartfelt 'not a dry eye in the house' '90s version of colonialism … No apology necessary. No land rights necessary.

Fallon is appalled that the birth of a white child is used as a device to 'dispel the ghosts of the black dead and despatch them to oblivion'. So desperate is Australia to make some reparation for our history that we cling to anyone who can tell us that it's alright that the cat is dead, it was just an accident, or the sort of misbehaviour that children are likely to engage in. Children grow out of it, don't they? Certainly. But the cat doesn't.

Fallon thinks *Cloudstreet* is popular because it 'delivers on John Howard's promise to make Australians feel comfortable and relaxed again'. That is a chilling comment on Australian letters, considering that the book was a clear winner in the *Australian Book Review*'s Favourite Australian Novel poll of 2010. Even since then, Australia can't get enough of the blockbuster novel, and the stage play and film it spawned. Critic Fiona Scott Norman remarked that in the reception of the play, 'every interview, every article speaks of this giant, lumbering beast of a show with wonder, joy and proud surprise'. Australia saved at last from its own history!

Perhaps the crowd of readers and reviewers should have asked a black person what she thought. At the Aboriginal Writers and Educators Conference at Wollongong in May 2011, a panel examined Winton's ingenuous excuses and that yearning Australia has to see itself in the best possible light – a nation of knockabout larrikin mates who don't take themselves too seriously and are not prepared to chew the rag of regret. Winton's great get-out-of-jail card was that all the black characters are dead. You don't have to depict them as realistic individuals, it's sufficient to re-invent their dreams!

The panellists did not heap scorn on Winton – some referred to their love of most of his books – but they were stunned by Australia's inability to notice his sleight of hand when it came to colonial history. Sleight of hand, after all, is just an entertaining form of deceit and theft.

The conversation moved on almost reluctantly to Kate Grenville's *The Secret River*. The panellists had grown up with Grenville's *Joan Makes History* and you could feel their disinclination to be critical of a feminist writer. But it has to be said that while the blacks in *The Secret River* are more alive than in *Cloudstreet*, their personalities have been cut from cardboard. On one of the few occasions a black man speaks, he uses the word 'hereabouts', which makes a linguistic first in my experience. At the end of the novel, the hero, Thornhill, peers across the valley to the cliffs and hopes to see a black man there, but they are gone and Thornhill has done the goneing. Thornhill is a much more nuanced character than Winton's Sam Pickles and acknowledges that he built his wealth on the backs of dead black people; he acknowledges it, but that's the only thing that separates him from the banality and crude intelligence of Sam Pickles. It is as if our most famous novels are trying to smooth the pillow of the dying race.

In the discussion, David Malouf's *Remembering Babylon* was compared to *The Secret River* because its tone of regret is prominent, but I was alarmed that I couldn't recollect much about Aboriginal people in the novel. As soon as I got home I read it again. It was a much better book than I remembered, but the 'black' character is not black at all but a 'lost' white sailor. Malouf makes an attempt at colonial analysis, but not one Aboriginal person speaks in the entire length of the text.

One of Malouf's heroines muses on the lack of ghosts in Australia, and a character believes that one day Australia will become one of God's gardens, that colonisation can have a divine purpose. The characters are reflective and serious, and their inability to 'see' the country is an irony, but the 'blacks' are absent, and no amount of musing on the delicious dusk described on the last page can bring them back.

The Wiradjuri educator and academic Jeanine Leane thinks that both Patrick White and David Malouf 'created white Indigenes ... which allows Aboriginality to be read as a "state" which can be achieved by settlers ... and then the "stealing" becomes a non-issue'. The white man usurps the black once again. *Remembering Babylon* might be a better book than I remembered, but it is not about black Australia or even, in any convincing way, Australian history.

I thought it was time I re-read Patrick White. I wrote in my book *Convincing Ground* of the dreadful pastiche of Aboriginal life in *A Fringe of Leaves*, but thought I should take another look at *Voss*, which had received a fair old serve in Wollongong.

You don't have to read too far. The black characters are fascinated by and covetous of brass buttons, they sulk rather than think, they are all inarticulate and suspicious, they speak gibberish, they are devious and untrustworthy and don't deserve a capital for Aboriginal.

Voss believes he must rule over his black subjects and notices that they aren't as awed and reverential of comets as white people. Some of these observations are made in Voss's delirium, but earlier descriptions of Aborigines offer no hope that White thought any differently. These characters are simply placed in the novel, not as figures of influence, but in order for White to use otherness to discuss the intellectualism of Europeans.

Rodney Hall's Yandilli Trilogy has blackfellas standing around on one leg, but they are there to allow for white analysis. Hall is a good writer and not 'against' Aboriginal Australia; it is just that his fascination lies elsewhere. White is like that too: he uses Aboriginal characters to shine light on European eminences. When speaking of black Australia he imagines the Aboriginal world rather than knows it. 'Such unimpaired innocence could only be the most devoted,' Voss muses on observing his black retainer. But there is never an attempt to explain why the black character stays with Voss on the doomed expedition; it is simply not important to White's story. The book is a determined allegory on man's search for meaning, but it is a European search for meaning with which White is concerned.

Riders in the Chariot was one of my favourite novels when I first read it, but on re-reading I noticed that the character of Alf Dubbo is given an Aboriginal heritage for narrative convenience. He is not a believable black character; he is purely a vehicle for White's theory of the outsider, which allows the mostly white Alf to have mystical thoughts and travel into the dark spaces of Australian geography.

For White and Voss, and most Australians for that matter, the desert is 'a devilish country', but the same desert that Voss (based on explorer Friedrich 'Ludwig' Leichhardt) traversed is where the almost dying explorer Charles Sturt was revived by Aborigines who fed him duck and offered him water from an eighty-foot well. This area is only a *desert* in so far as Australians view any country that can't grow wheat or mineralise iron oxide as worthless.

The Wollongong conference became strained as Aboriginal and non-Aboriginal wrestled with the literature of our shared country. When a comment from the floor offered the view that some of Patrick White's best friends were black, it was greeted with scarifying levity. There was no nastiness in the mirth; it is just that Aboriginal people have learned to fear most white Australians who claim Aboriginals as 'some of their best friends' or that they 'grew up with Aborigines and know how they think'.

When Katherine Susannah Prichard's *Coonardoo* was published in 1929, left-wing commentators hailed it as a landmark text on black–white relations. Prichard was the first novelist to attempt the characterisation of an Aboriginal individual – but Coonardoo is a hapless woman who cannot think for herself, and she *pales* in comparison to the strong, white characters wrestling with their anxiety, their responsibility for blacks, their destiny.

Left-wing critics also loved Eve Langley's *The Pea Pickers* without seeming to realise that pea picking in southern Australia was dominated by poor Aboriginal families. In Langley's novel the pea paddock is a stage for European labourers to practise equality and for women to demand it. Despite the real history of the industry, only a few lines refer to Aboriginal people, and those lines drip with contempt.

Nino Culotta's (John O'Grady's) *They're a Weird Mob* sold 130,000 copies in its first year of publication, 1957, and eventually sold more than one million copies in a country with a population of fifteen million. What was the attraction? It told the story of an Italian migrant assimilating into Australian society who urged his fellow migrants to do the same. They're a weird mob, but they're terrific blokes! (Women hardly rated a mention in the book.)

Australians loved the book because they loved the representation of themselves as humorous, knockabout, generous blokes who were kind to the new arrivals. It's a pretty telling profile of Australians in the 1950s and 1960s that such a book was wildly popular. The danger of such books is that they airbrush the national portrait and paper over the cracks with images that could have been taken from Ken Done and Pro Hart: innocent pictures of beaches and palms, yachts with colourful sails, quaintly rickety sheds and hardened Aussie bush folk who are tanned and not black.

As a youth I yearned for a national literature that was truly about Australia, and before I found Patrick White I got all whimsical about the poetry of Henry Kendall and Charles Harpur, simply because they *mentioned* bellbirds and blackfellas. I'd almost forgotten about that teenage love affair until Jeanine Leane explained that Harpur would don blackface to read his poetry to gushing audiences.

As a student and later a teacher of literature, I continued to search for a novel that could get within a southern swampland of William Faulkner's unabashed love of country and its people. By the 1970s Xavier Herbert's *Poor Fellow My Country* came closest to Faulknerite depth and scope, but on re-reading I found the book was dominated by conversations between numerous white characters and that the protagonist, a wandering chemist, was much like Herbert himself. The Aboriginal people are drawn in greater depth than in many other novels of the time, but these characters are incapable of taking positive action to defend themselves without the intervention of an imbibing chemist. In Herbert's later novel, *Capricornia,* the mixed-blood son of a white man is a stain on the character of the protagonist, and the unsuitability of the dark stain is reinforced throughout the book.

Barbara Baynton's coruscating stories have true depth, but she had given up on Aboriginal Australia. At least she was honest about her opinion. On the other hand, Mary Durack's epic *Kings in Grass Castles* is among the worst apologies for European atrocities this country has seen, but is still regarded by many as fair-minded towards Aboriginal peoples. Perhaps any Australian writer who simply *mentions* Aboriginal Australia is deemed to have been generous.

When I read Patrick White's *The Tree of Man* in 1964, it was the first time I recognised the bush of my childhood. Alan Marshall's love of the bush was obvious, and Henry Lawson's yearning for the misty blue ranges of loneliness infected my soul, but it was White's majestic use of language that unfurled the scrolled bark of the land where I lived. White taught me that there was a reputable Australian literature to compare with the works of Joseph Conrad, William Faulkner and Leo Tolstoy. And so, after finishing all White's novels and plays, I turned to Eleanor Dark's *The Timeless Land* and saw there a grander story and a deeper love of the land and was drawn into its tale.

But when I picked it up again a few years back, I was left wanting for descriptions of Aboriginal Australians other than as remote figures on the horizon. Indigenous figures weren't always standing on one leg, but while their story was told with resignation and regret, it wasn't told from the Aboriginal point of view. Maybe that's because one of the great Australian claims for innocence is that many among the white population pretend not to know any Aboriginals. We maintain this myth as an explanation for our bemused sorrow, and yet if you passed two hundred people in Sydney's Pitt Street or Melbourne's Bourke Street this morning, it is likely that six of them would have been Aboriginal. Australia doesn't recognise the Aboriginal past or the Aboriginal face.

Do all countries have such a conflicted relationship with their history, and do all countries want nations around the world to love them as desperately as does Australia? I suspect the Americans are blinded by stars and stripes. The Italians, with former heads of state such as Silvio Berlusconi, have surely gone beyond expecting respect. And countries such as Israel and Iran are so involved with the preservation of their authority that they have learnt not to trust the world's opinion.

Colonial countries all rewrite their history, but not all forget it entirely. William Faulkner took the scalpel to the culture and society of America's Deep South, but it's interesting that he had very little to say about Native Americans. Peter Mathieson spent his best words on the relationship between America and its freed slaves, as did the mighty John Steinbeck. Only in Australia has avoidance of any unpleasantness become a major literary theme. As a result we end up painting beach scenes in miniature; nice little Rupert Bunnys.

Australians do not want to be perceived as racist thieves – who would? – but we yearn with frustrated desperation for respectability, and so we are doomed to choose as our public symbols only those things untainted by the past: Don Bradman and Fred Hollows, Mary McKillop and the Drover's Wife. It is inevitable that in this fog of identity we make icons of the novels that persuade us we have 'dealt' with our colonial history and overcome it.

We also contort ourselves in every national conversation on the subject. Australian pioneers had to forget about the theft and murder if they wanted to remain good Christian blokes, but the current generation has invented new forms of self-deceit to avoid contemplation of the real national story. We *had* to intervene. We *had* to employ the methods we know failed in 1880. And today: we *have* to save them from their debased selves.

Like the child rationalising the dead cat, in the panic to explain ourselves and our history, we often point the finger at other naughty children – like those 'black' others who are pointing the finger at us. We deflect attention from our sins. The people asking us to revisit our history are not 'real' Aborigines, the argument goes; they are members of the guilt industry, or simply cut from a lesser intellectual cloth.

The time when we could survive as an intelligent nation while believing the Little Golden Book of our history has passed. We consider it an unthinkable cruelty to bind the feet of women to restrict and imprison them, but it is no less cruel to bind and blind the mind to the obvious truths of our heritage. The national heart is compressed, and its generosity coldly selective. It is natural to want to belong to good, honest parents and a good, honest country, it is natural to want to be considered moral – in fact, it is our saving grace – but we cannot build our individual and national castle on the sands of a fabricated history.

Any nation's artists and thinkers set the tone and breadth of national conversations. Politicians only choose the electable catch-phrase: 'stop the boats' or 'save the little children'. It is up to the thinkers and artists if we are to develop a deep, respectful, endur-ing and fully aware love of our country.

There is much to learn about the past, but Australia tore those pages from our history books because they mention the broken commandments of our Lord. We all have to bite the bullet of our history or we will be condemned to self-congratulation for the rest of our lives – a nation without modesty, without compas-sion, a spoilt and selfish people forever chortling about goodness and mateship. It is infantile for an adult to keep rearranging the dead cat and blaming it for our sin. One can feign incomprehen-sion of, and memory loss about, the past for only so long before it becomes a national characteristic for which we will be continually judged. If Australia cannot learn about the past and the descend-ants of those who once owned the land, it is doomed to a shallow, friable national intelligence. Where there is sand, there is little rock.

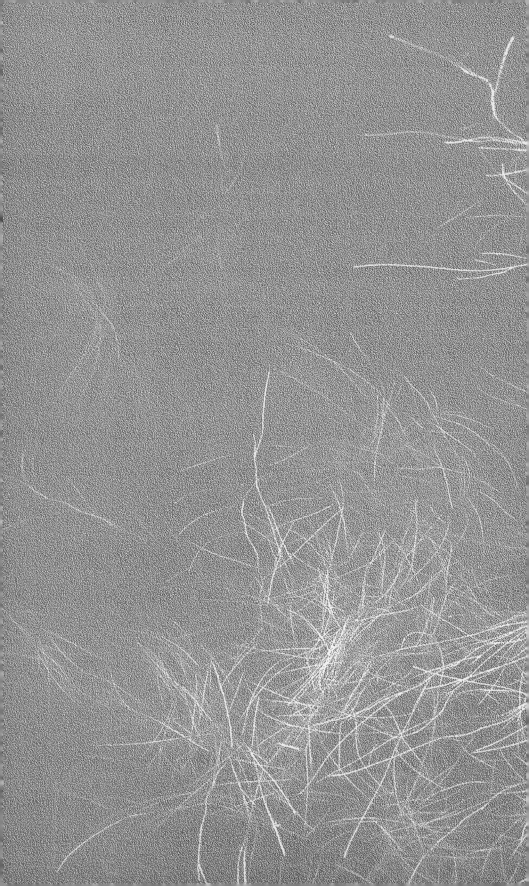

SEA WOLVES

SEA WOLVES

Three hours before dawn, twenty-five naked men crouched and shivered in the blasted heath of Baran Guba, an island off the south coast of New South Wales. The massive granite plinths of Guruwul, the whale, and Narangga, the shark, loomed against the black sky and the sea wolves howled.

Wedge-tailed shearwaters blundered through the heath, colliding with the men who, locked in darkness, had no idea what spirits were assailing them. And they were spirits – spirits of *gadu*, the ocean. Their voices began at four a.m., at first as tentative contact calls: *way coo, way coo; I am here, so am I, me too, way coo, way coo.* Then they projected their voices in long wails, an ancient ululation exactly like the howl of a wolf, a sound preparing the birds for their day coursing the crests of waves in hunt for small fish skipping and darting on the surface of *gadu*. But first they had to gain momentum before launching themselves into the darkness, and collision with crouching Yuin men was the least of their concerns; they were seeking the wind's clear air and the cushion it provided between them and the ocean's surface. They glided and curved against that cushion for the entire day, and when they leave these shores they will ride it for months.

I could see my son's head as he crouched in that heath and I knew he had no idea what awaited him, but it was too late to wonder. He was about to become a man.

I didn't cry. I had done that the day before, when I told him who he was in relation to the whale. Before he was born, his parents stood in a cave above a Bass Strait bay sheltering from the rain, and a rock appeared in the sea where none had been before. Barnacles crusted the mass and the surge of *gadu* swept over it, but suddenly she reared eight metres above the waves and presented herself to us: Guruwul the whale. For two hours we watched that whale as she swam in a giant ellipse to the horizon, and back into the shallows of the Parker River with her half-sized companion. She was teaching her calf to swim.

I put my hand on the woman's belly and felt my son roll like a miniature leviathan. He was Guruwul, and the day before the sea wolves moaned in the pre-dawn pitch he had received that name. No wonder I doubled over and tears sprang from my eyes; the great circle of the whale along the coast was complete.

The old man behind me on that day had been initiated by a man whose father did not have an English name. Of course, the 'settlers' shot that man, and his wife and forty others of his family. Only the boy remained, and he was 'taken' by a man called Hammond, who had been involved in the incident. The son of that boy, Muns Hammond, lived to be 115 years old, and so the men crouched in the heath of Baran Guba received a cultural legacy handed down in an unbroken line from way before European occupation of the continent.

I am related to that old man in the convoluted way typical of the massive disruption of Aboriginal families, and the survival of such a small number since the colonial period means that most Aboriginal people of the south coast are descended from fewer than sixty or so individuals.

Despite that disruption, however, the culture has survived and remembers all the incidents of our dispossession. Australian Aboriginal culture has not been 'washed away by the tide of history' but remains vivid in black minds and acts as the locus for our lives.

Many Australians pretend they have never met an Aboriginal person despite Aboriginals and Torres Strait Islanders comprising 3 per cent of the population. It's not that we are scarce but that Australians do not recognise an Aboriginal face. Perhaps that face is unremarkable because a large number of Australians share it as a result of the absence of white women in the early years of colonisation.

In a commentary in *The Age*, Waleed Aly wondered about Australia's vicious response to the most polite suggestion that our nation was invaded rather than settled. Intelligent people contort their thinking to construct sophist arguments to reassure Australia that it has an innocent, even heroic, history.

There was a war for possession of the soil. Aboriginal people lost it. Aboriginal people did engage in primary production and sophisticated models of government. Australians turned their backs on this evidence in the colonial era and deny it today. An inconvenient truth for a Christian country devoted to the idea of the Ten Commandments rather than their application to political life and private rumination.

This history is incredibly close to us, not a remote and hazy confusion but a real and palpable fact. We can still see the foundations of large houses burnt down as a routine policy by settlers anxious to gild their land grab with legitimacy. We can still see the massive canal systems cut through stone to farm eels. We can still see the dams built by Aboriginal people even if we have to remove the extensions added by Europeans. We can still see the arms of ancient fish traps on tourist beaches, and we can still see the four pieces of the massive granite spire that proclaimed to the entire Bega Valley that Baiame was looking over them.

The history has not gone away – we just choose not to see it.

When I was researching *Convincing Ground* and *Dark Emu,* I was told by senior historians that every primary document in the Australian history trove had been thoroughly examined; there was nothing new to be discovered. I wondered about that confidence as I sat in the State Library of Victoria and cut the pages of a memoir that had never been opened. I wondered about contemporary historians' belief that Aboriginal residents of Cape Otway numbered no more than eight when a local resident informed me that his grandfather's letters and diaries recounted one of the massacres in the region as accounting for twenty Aboriginal lives.

As a guide at Cape Otway Lighthouse, I was always delighted to talk with French, German, Italian and Vietnamese tourists. They could never believe Australia's accepted version of history and were hungry for information about the colonial war and Aboriginal culture. They needed it to make sense of the country. Australians, on the other hand, were jittery at the mere mention of the land war, and scornful when shown the delicate stone tools of the Gadubanud. One stone, and I hope it is still there, served as a needle-sharpening device, a thread cutter and a measure. It is smaller than a matchbox but serves a multitude of purposes. Overseas tourists understand its significance immediately, while many Australians express scorn. *Just looks like a rock to me. Why didn't they invent the wheel?*

Perhaps the people who invented egalitarian government and practised it for 120,000 years didn't have the imagination to devise a transportation device for cannons. Perhaps the people who invented bread were looking at life from a different perspective.

Thirty-six thousand years ago a woman collected a handful of seeds and looked at them. Maybe she lay awake that night, pondering the potential of the little grains. Whatever she did, once she had confirmed her suspicions she added water and heat to the flour and invented bread. It's probable that the invention is much older than 36,000 years but we're not sure because we've only expended the intellectual effort to DNA-test one grinding dish from Cuddie Springs.

What we do know about that woman is that she conducted this alchemy 17,000 years before the next woman on earth who tried it. That other woman lived in Egypt, where we still send our best and brightest archaeologists to investigate the pyramids, a task as important as one more critical text on Shakespeare's *Macbeth*. Our best engineers are engaged in plans for the construction of freeways and coal-fired power stations that will never be built, while the four parts of the Biamanga Mountain monolith still lie on the ground, where they fell after the explosion that paved the way for the ugly asbestos hut housing a radio transmitter that has long since ceased operation.

I dream of finding a million dollars to airlift those pieces back into place so that Baiame might again declare his vision of peace for the entire south-eastern corner of Australia. I dream of finding $4000 to scrape the sand away from the Bermagui fish trap so that Aboriginal people can utilise its efficiency to secure their economic future.

These are not big sums of money. They are dwarfed by the bribes Leighton Holdings paid to secure contracts in the oilfields of Iraq, a country our then prime minister insisted had to be invaded because it had weapons of mass destruction.

Afghanistan, Palestine, Sudan, Ethiopia, Georgia, the Amazon and Costa Rica could all use the pacification wrought by sensitive government based on fairness rather than religious bigotry or greed. Australia had that form of government and refuses to acknowledge this for the peevish reason that it requires us to reflect on how we came to possess the soil.

Those old Aboriginal people must have anguished over their social design. Here we are in a dry continent, they must have thought. How can we ensure that it provides sufficient food for all? How can we ensure everyone has enough to eat, a house, care when aged or if handicapped, an education that gives every child a chance to learn about her world? I know those ideas are revolutionary and today would be treated as some kind of communist plot, but they worked. The only firm basis on which to condemn them is to conclude that an elite minority deserve a million times more food and wealth than the majority.

I have visited the world's finest galleries and churches. I have sat beneath golden domes, passed through the gem-studded doors of grand mansions. I have walked slowly past the world's most famous art and pondered the swords, the boiling oil, the rack, the torture of infidels, the glorification of paedophile priests and kings, and never failed to be transported back to my own culture, where instead of men ruling the world with violence, women are central; where men cannot speak without first saying the words *Bingyadyan gnallu birrung nudjarn jungarung*: we arise from the mother's heartbeat. It's a declaration of the primacy of women.

Instead of rampant lions and elephants, kings dripping in jewels and holding aloft golden swords, our people see the power-brokers of the world as the blue wren and the emu wren. The Ganai people of East Gippsland play football with those two birds emblazoned on their jumpers. *Come on, the Wrens!* The Yuin see the black duck as pivotal to their life, gaze upon the representation of its form in Wallaga Lake and feel secure.

There are depictions in Aboriginal art of the killer boomerang and the spear in association with imprecations about the importance of keeping the lore, but the dominant images are gentle: a row of bats hanging from a tree to teach us about the importance of family; fish and kangaroos to teach us about conservation; beings floating in space with their legs folded back at the knee to impress upon us the importance of dream and the wonders it reveals.

Our culture's reliance on agriculture is even displayed in the names we give ourselves. The people of the interior often called themselves *Panara* or derivatives of that word because it means grass; that is, we are the people who harvest grass seed. The Darug of western Sydney called themselves after the name of the yam, the staple of their diet.

Aboriginal song is replete with the importance of preparing and sharing food. Women of the centre dance with a repetitive action representing the broadcast of seed, women south and east of the Great Dividing Range dance with their yam sticks.

Young people today clamour to be allowed to join those dances. There was a time when the church and state repressed that cultural ambition, but it is alive today, and I attend every performance I can where the Djajawan dancers appear, simply to see older women dance with three generations of their womenfolk.

I have danced where the oldest participant was eighty-three and the youngest was thirteen. We danced for the shark, the black duck, the whale and the lyrebird. As we entered one cultural precinct, the clapsticks announced the arrival of every of the twenty-nine individuals. The lyrebird immediately repeated the sound and tempo perfectly. Twenty-nine times. All twenty-nine of us burst into laughter conjured by the irony of a bird honouring our culture.

The lyrebird imitates other birds and animals, machines, cameras and whistling kettles, and passes those songs down to each generation. One lyrebird in the Macedon Ranges is still repeating the sound of a camera shutter, which it probably hasn't heard for fifteen years. The lyrebird's default call is this: clapsticks. It has remembered the rituals of our old people and continues to entertain itself and prospective partners with that sound. On Gulaga Mountain there's a lyrebird that has begun to hear that sound again and launches into its repetition every time it hears the sticks being played. It has a brother on Biamanga Mountain who does the same thing, seemingly delighted to hear again what it previously had to guard as a cultural memory.

Lyrebirds remember and respect our culture, even if most Australians do not.

While I was writing this, I was aware of the nostalgia bordering on sorrow that I was tapping onto the board, but in reality it is the mildest of griefs because I must be among the most fortunate of men, if you consider the sorrow, misfortune and pain the majority on earth have to survive. But there is nostalgia and there is grief nonetheless.

On that island I was teaching young men how to knap stone to make blades and chisels. Fortunately none of them had any greater skills than my sketchy ones, but we struggled away, compared techniques and results, and edged towards a method of some utility. We were conscious that beside us on the rock were remnants of stone manufacture that must have been at least 200 years old, and some that we knew were only four years old. We were on a vast granite slab that Yuin men had used over a longer time than the duration of any human construction on earth. We mused on the antiquity of this heritage, aware that we, no matter the relative crudeness of our craft, were continuing it.

I left the men on the rock to retrieve a tool from the camp and was immediately transfixed by the activity there. A group were fashioning wooden implements with a mixture of stone and steel tools. One young man was teaching an even younger man dance steps. Two other men were cooking fish they'd caught off the rocks, and two old men reclined in the shade, talking about the next stage of cultural teaching. Somewhere else, a man was learning a song while another accompanied him on clapsticks he'd made himself. I didn't stop my progress through the camp, but I was shaken by the cultural pulse.

The previous day I'd gone chasing my son so we could dive together, to repeat a habit that we'd indulged in for most of our lives, but when I couldn't find the cove where he was fishing with other Gurandgi I swam in the first likely bay and was joined by two seals who must have learned to associate men with fish.

It was a glorious and tranquil swim, and I left the water refreshed but pensive. I trudged back along a grassy island lane, and at an intersection I met four other Gurandgi who had been to the far side of the island to inspect cultural sites. We looked at each other and became still, each of us conscious of our state. This must have been what it was always like. Men, because women never visited that island, of a camp engaged in the multifarious tasks of the cultural economy, meeting as they returned to camp. It seemed so natural, so ancient, even if one of the near-naked men wore a watch and another carried a plastic mask and snorkel and a nylon mesh bag full of shellfish.

That mood of pensive wonder stayed with me for five days, until I nearly stepped into the path of a car on Merimbula's main street on Easter Monday. It wasn't sadness, not even morbid nostalgia, that had rendered me so insensible to the 'real' world, but mere surprise at the quickness with which we could revert to the tempo of that old life.

You might think that 'Stone Age' skills are less than useful in the information age, but it is the investigation of those old skills that teaches us more than the 'quaint' technology of the past. We learnt about a living tempo and recognised elements of the cultural stories that were rooted in just that rhythm and the contemplation for which it allowed room. And the springboard for that learning was the country itself. No page in any library can provide comparable stimulation. Every morning on the island I woke at 4.00 a.m. to the sea wolves making contact with one another, *way coo, way coo, yowooocroo ow,* and knew that the old people had woken to the same sound at this time of the year, and some of the songs and words they had left us were designed to describe that eerie pre-dawn ritual: members of an avian clan greeting one another.

This might sound mournful and tinged with grief, but really

there was a kind of wild joy in the realisation that we were still able to enter that old and infinitely gentle culture.

The riches of the oldest human culture on earth are available to Australians; very little of it is prohibited to the uninitiated or to those of a different race. Most of it can become the reassuringly comfortable garb of all Australians. We're not inviting a second dispossession of our culture but an awakening of the nation to the land itself. We can all love it and care for it; we can love and care for each other. This is not a return to Rousseauian gloom but an awareness of our country and its needs and ours. We need non-Aboriginal Australians to love the land. We must not quell the impulse to see the bush and the beaches as any Australian's heritage because without that identification with the soil, those questing souls remain restless and dangerous spirits, uncommitted to the protection of the continent.

Any Australian can climb Gulaga Mountain and visit the seven chapters of Yuin lore. Women can walk to the summit if they wish, but men can go no higher than the gallery of granite tors. It is on the walk through those tors that the gentleness of Aboriginal culture is most apparent. You enter by the forms of Nyaardi, the woman; you pass Tunku, the man, who is second, and then you pass the pregnant woman, and it is culturally appropriate to rub her swollen belly. The next chapter is the baby being carried on its mother's back. Look at that child's eyes and, if you are a parent, allow yourself to be engulfed by the memory of your own children's births. Where are the swords and war machines, where are the gilded halls of selfish men, where are the severed heads of people who disagreed with the king? On Gulaga Mountain you are invited to rub the belly of a pregnant woman.

I never fail to be moved by the gentleness of my culture and never fail to wish that the directionless among the men of our people could muster the energy to climb the mountain barefoot to absorb the profound respect our old people had for women. This is not just a lesson for Aboriginal men but for men across the planet. Do not climb the mountain if you want to revisit a quaint and forgotten culture – but if you want to contemplate a world without war, that sees women as the centre of civilisation, this is the place to go. You can be guided to it by Yuin men and women who share the lineage of those who insisted that this was the destiny of humans and saw that story writ in stone. It will cost you less than a speeding fine.

That gentleness extends beyond women to the land itself, and surely now we can see that respect and care for our soil and waters is in our own selfish interests.

We can keep our computers, and for at least another twenty years we can keep our cars, but we can also contemplate the Murray River and the outlandish idea that it is within our capacity to make sure there is water in it. We can contemplate the Biamanga granite spire and the petroglyphic 'bible' at Burrup Peninsula and realise we can enjoy a rich standard of living and keep these representations of the human spirit at its profound and elegant best.

You don't have to be Aboriginal to understand Burrup art or listen to the sea wolf shearwaters, but it would serve you well to understand Aboriginal philosophy if you wanted to save them and the land on which they exist. We cannot leave such momentous decisions to the craven and vindictive legion of red and blue politicians fascinated by the prospect of their own survival. We are Australians; it is we who have the power. And the philosophy required to generate that power already exists in this land, and is available to us should we decide to embrace it rather than the swamis and gurus of India or the chanting and floating flowers of Buddhist temples. All we need to do is to acknowledge its existence, and that, of course, is through history.

TOO UPSETTING

One hundred and thirty dollars buys you a six-hour World Heritage Cruise – including a 'sumptuous' lunch – out of the west Tasmanian town of Strahan, across Macquarie Harbour and along the Gordon River.

The tour commentary is constant, about Bob Hawke and Bob Brown's fight to save the Franklin River from the hydro-electricity engineers, about the high quality of the salmon produced in the local fish farms (and their owners' fortunes), about the domestic details of the prisoners and guards at the Sarah Island convict settlement, even about an officer's indiscretion with a very attractive goat.

As we pass 3000-year-old Huon pines, the guide describes how two men could cut down 1000 of these trees each year, how there were at least thirty such teams – 30,000 trees a year – and how those fellows battled once the pine was all gone. (Hell of a surprise.) Rapacious companies and the government sooled them on until the hills were bare and their mighty labour was no longer needed, after which they were sacked. (More surprise.)

There are many stories of these indefatigable piners, their horrific accidents, the leeches that assailed them and the women who loved them, but not once are the words 'Aboriginal' or 'Indigenous' mentioned. The closest we get, and I listen intently, is the phrase 'the first white men on that river'. That inconspicuous phrase is tantalising. There may have been men of other colour on the river.

Evidence of Indigenous Tasmanians has been found up and down the island's west coast. There are the whalebone house constructions, the cooking ovens, the fishing machines, the whale etchings older than any other art in the world apart from that of mainland Australia. And yet their labours, their injuries, their loving women, their contest with the leeches, and their industry are of no interest on this wonderful craft.

I did appreciate the guide's story of the logger who rowed nonstop for fourteen hours to get help for the axe wound in his brother's leg. I hoped that we would segue from that story to the master boatwomen and -men of the Gordon, and the curatorial cray-fisherwomen of the west coast.

As we hoed into the locally farmed salmon, boutique cheeses and beers – I can devour seafood, camembert and Boag's along with the rest, polish my plate and look around for more – was it too much to hope for even a scrap about the first people to inhabit the harbour and river?

Later, I scour Strahan's information centre, a vast barn of Huon pine memorabilia and nightly re-enactments, but find no mention of whale petroglyphs there either. Nor on Bruny Island, south of Hobart, where I go to look for the whale songline.

Not one person I meet at any of the information centres can provide a single shred of information, nor can any of the glossy brochures for cheese, wine, salmon, oysters, bread, art and lawn bowls. Whales? Cultureline? How curious.

There are some people who sense the direction of my search and their jaws harden, like that of a boatman who has been rowing for fourteen hours.

Aboriginal people still perform ceremonies to welcome the whale, to thank him for regurgitating his lore onto the land. But apparently a living cultureline, tens of thousands of years old, that begins at Hervey Bay in Queensland and goes all the way to Albany in Western Australia is of little historical import when compared with convicts, bestial officers and old kerosene lamps.

Most Australians know about Burke and Wills, and Hargraves' discovery of gold. But few know that Aboriginal people tried to save Burke's silly life before he began to shoot at them, or that Hargraves was not the first to find gold. Locals had known about the metal for tens of thousands of years but had decided not to gild religious domes with it, slaughter for it or scrooge it away. Perhaps most Australians prefer not to know.

I admit that I sat curmudgeonly in my cruise-ship seat, watching schoolchildren on the forward deck allow the wind created by our thirty-two knots of progress to fill their parkas so that they all looked like Michelin kids. Even I, in my grumpiness, couldn't deny them their hilarity, their exhilaration at braving the elements. But I would have liked to pose a few questions to them after they had come inside to fill themselves with chips and fizzy drinks. I would have liked to talk to them about other families on other exquisitely designed craft, when other children shrieked in delight at the bracing wind and the waves slapping the sides of their canoes.

But we ran out of time. There's only so much history that can be revealed in six hours.

WATER HARVEST

When one of the early sailing ships limped around Victoria's Cape Otway after a vicious storm in Bass Strait, the captain was astounded to find numerous canoes fishing in benign waters in the lee of the Cape. All the canoes were sailed by Gadabanud women.

The occupation of Montague Island, nine kilometres off the coast of New South Wales at Narooma, had to be negotiated by canoe, as sea levels were never sufficiently low to make it accessible by land. One of the enduring stories told by the local people is of a terrible calamity when a fleet of canoes was overwhelmed by a sudden squall as they returned from the island.

Lady Julia Percy Island, ten kilometres off the Victorian coast, near Portland, was also inaccessible, even during low sea-level periods. However, it was occupied extensively by Aboriginal people, who called it Deen Maar.

Watercraft were a significant tool in the Aboriginal and Torres Strait Island economy. Rottnest Island, eighteen kilometres off the Western Australian coast from Fremantle, could be reached by land around 120,000 years ago. However, some of the artefacts currently under examination by archaeologists are reputed to be

60,000 years old. Ocean voyages must have been undertaken to reach the island under the lure of the enormous seafood resources.

In arguably his most evocative writing, George Augustus Robinson compared the night fleets fishing on the Murray to the harbour at Teneriffe, while homesteader Andrew Beveridge said of the fleets he observed, '[T]he flotilla presented a scene so quaintly striking as to be well worthy of an artist's pencil.' Canoes with outriggers were built in the north of the country and in the Torres Strait Islands, and were seen well out to sea hunting for pelagic fish. Small sails were also used for ocean canoes when line and net fishing. On inland waterways, canoes were employed as punts to cross rivers, and were often described by explorers as the only way they could continue their adventures of discovery. Many early photographs of Australian waterways feature various canoe designs and the nets and traps associated with them.

Yuin people of the New South Wales south coast have reintroduced the canoe-making tradition; several fine examples have been produced, including one made on the banks of the Brogo River.

When I visited members of the Pascoe family at Lockhart River on the Cape York Peninsula in 2009, I was struck by the number of people involved in the fishing industry. Every backyard seemed to have a tinny. Those east coast Cape communities have vegetable and fruit products in the jungles and on the plains, and harvest them still, but their eyes are forever turned to the sea.

Author Stephanie Anderson translated a terrific book about the French sailor Pelletier, who was cast away on this part of the coast in 1858 and lived for some time with the local Aboriginals. Hints of early reliance on the produce from the sea can be found in this account. Pelletier also discusses the people's management of yam production to ensure a supply during the dry season, but it is the sea from which those people gained most of their nutrition and cultural solace.

The early history of Australia is crowded with references to Aboriginal watercraft and fishing techniques, yet Australians remain strangely impervious to that knowledge, and to the Aboriginal economy in general.

*　　*　　*

The Australian coast, from just south of Perth, across the southern coast, including Tasmania and her islands, west to Gippsland in eastern Victoria and north to Wollongong in New South Wales, supported the Aboriginal abalone harvest.

The skeletons of women from Victoria's coastal regions were found to have an odd bone growth in the ear. Scientists recognised that the bone had thickened to protect the ear from extreme cold; the women had been abalone divers. They had what doctors refer to as 'surfers' ear'.

Diving for crayfish and abalone was an important part of the southern coastal economy. Not all the diving was done by women, but in Tasmania and Victoria the shellfish was collected predominantly by women.

Uncle Banjo Clarke, a Keeraywoorrong Elder, described to me the process by which men netted and speared crayfish. The most intriguing fact was how men would swim to a reef and hang onto the kelp while nudging with their feet for the feelers of a crayfish. They would then dive down and grab the feelers, and haul the crayfish from its cave.

Access to large fish resources was common in Australia, and the methods employed to harvest them varied. Some resources were so productive that they allowed many communities to live a sedentary or semi-sedentary life close to their fish traps or their fishing grounds.

Women from the Eden area in southern New South Wales have written a book, *Mutton Fish*, chronicling the Yuin and neighbouring First Nations reliance on the abalone economy. The shellfish was a favoured high-protein item of the coastal diet in this part of Australia.

The shell of the abalone is beautifully coloured rainbow pearl. It was used in the making of traditional jewellery, but breaks down very quickly and is under-represented in living site remains as a result. The shells of turbo (*warrener*) or blood mussels (*bimbula*) are much more prevalent, although they probably represent a fraction of the protein yield.

Archaeologists can only measure what they find, so soft-skeleton and friable-shell creatures such as crayfish, whiting, shark, abalone, urchin and snapper are often under-represented in surveys of the Aboriginal maritime economy. European settlers shunned the abalone, referring to it derogatorily as 'mutton fish'. English cooking has never enjoyed much of a reputation, and so the colonial chefs applied their most subtle method to the abalone: boiling. The flesh of the abalone takes on the texture of industrial rubber when handled this way, and so the 'mutton fish' was considered food for 'blacks'. The Chinese and Japanese knew otherwise. They pounded the fish, sliced it finely and cooked it quickly – for no more than thirty seconds – in a searing pan. Treated this way, the flesh is delicate, tender and full of flavour.

One Aboriginal recipe suggests cooking the abalone in its own shell on hot coals. I tried this, expecting the flesh to toughen under these conditions, but instead found that it remained tender and even more flavourful.

Once entrepreneurs realised that Australian Chinese were exporting abalone meat, they lobbied the state departments of primary industry to establish licensing, quotas and closed marketing boards, which operated like cartels.

Aboriginal people are now seen as poachers simply because the shellfish is so valuable. When it was 'mutton fish', they were allowed to harvest as much as they wanted. Today they are jailed for pursuing their traditional harvest.

THE UNAPPROVED DAY

I wasn't poaching. Not really. But because thieves are abroad, restrictions have been placed on the collection of abalone that only became valuable because the Japanese think it is an aphrodisiac.

So I wasn't really poaching, just lifting my half-quota of abs, but on an unapproved day of the month. Oh, the blessedness of the unapproved day. I've had a few and they have been entirely glorious.

And this was the latest. Reclined in the patchy shade of a white berry bush and a dwarf boobialla on a sun-warmed rock. Green sandstone smooths to the wash of the sea and usually provides a small eroded dish to accommodate the hip, and another for the shoulder, and if you angle yourself properly there should be another to receive the head.

I can feel the warmth of the rock infusing my muscles. I'm naked, but nobody comes to this corner because you have to swim to it and there's no coffee bar within a stylish stroll.

I doze and dream and dream and doze, the sun a mesh of striated flares through my lashes. Ah, the unapproved day.

I have four abalone pressed together in pairs pretending they are still sucking to a rock. I've wrapped them in wet sacking. I saw four crayfish too, but they're far back in a deep ledge. I left two abalone for them, and they'll be fighting over these while I wait for the tide to fall. I have no pride, no honour; I am seducing a very stupid animal so I can pluck it from the cave and later drown it in fresh water and cook it, where it will glow cherry red from chagrin. Pardon me, southern rock, I'm a murderer.

I pick up the flippers, mask and snorkel, diving bag and gloves. Even thinking about the luxury of immersion, I tingle for the total watery embrace. I'm recharging here in the sun but dreaming of cool depths.

I sit on a rock at the edge of one of those magnificent pools where weeds and starfish, guppies and crabs, do a slow semaphore. Tiny black molluscs scrape indecisive runes on the sand-silted rock as I don the monster gear of the diver, a crude and unconvincing approximation of the seal.

I love the entry, the slide, the languorous glide as my weight belt makes me the equal of gravity and air and ocean. Wrasse and beautifully spangled pearl perch swivel their eyes to my grotesque impersonation so they can mock it later in their dark caverns. Man swimming, what a laugh!

The manta ray is in her personal trench, all but covered by sand, and only revealed by her horns protruding through the grit and broken shells of the ribbed sea floor.

As I approach the cave I'm sure my pulse would race if it wasn't for the sedation of the sea and the slow *frrrk, frrrk, frrrk* of the snorkel and the salt sluicing through my sinuses, the bony tubes below the skin of my face tranquilised, my whole being sung by deep silence.

The cave is just below me and I crawl down a long ribbon of kelp, hand over hand, to peer in where my spiky friends are slow-motion wrestling for possession of the abalone. Is it an intellectual life, the existence of a crayfish? Do they spend long cave hours contemplating the government's position on climate change? Observing this slow and irresolute wrestle for flesh, it is hard to believe quick thoughts pass between their horns. The crayfish, not the government.

One crusty red devil is reluctant to forfeit the feast, and I grab him by the feelers and stuff him in my sea bag, scoop up two snowy sea urchins and roll away from the cave. I rise in a lazy glide. I allow the swell to sweep me onto a reef covered in bubble weed and limpets. I drag the mask from my face and lie there, lifted and tumbled by the wash of waves, cradled by the sea.

My pride in this small victory is repulsive. Tonight I'll bring a luxury to the table. My wife will smile, and the efforts I am prepared to make to ensure she does this are sly and despicable. It is a very beautiful smile, and even to think of it makes my chest cave. It is certainly a guilty and reprehensible pleasure.

I crack an urchin with the ab steel and scoop out the orange roe, sliding it down my throat. They taste like salty tongues. One more for old time's sake, and I'm aquiver with pleasure.

The sun is a snare of blazing tendrils through salt-gummed lashes, and I allow this sea dream to lave my loins. I'm beyond all decency now. The sea's great heave is rocking and dandling me on one of her chosen rocks. She has tried to kill me twice, but not today, not on this unapproved day.

WHALE AND SERPENT

Bingyadyan gnallu birrung nudjarn jungarung.

A woman stood in a cave sheltering from the rain. A man stood beside her. She was pregnant. Heavily. They looked out at the bleak sea, grey like lead, moody, mean. They stared at it, waiting for the rain to stop. They knew this bay like they knew the path to their back door.

A reef appeared where none had been before. And grew and grew and grew until it loomed over the wave like a great tower. And there was an eye in the tower that swivelled to where the man and woman stood in the cave. The beast looked at them. Guruwul.

She sank below the wave and another smaller animal appeared at her side and the two swam away, out to the horizon, and the man and woman watched even though the rain had stopped and weak sunshine seeped through the clouds like the disappearance of tears. The whales returned to the bay and the man and woman saw the mother's eye watch them before it turned to the ocean again with its calf. They repeated this giant pelagic loop time and time again. She was teaching her calf to swim and sift the ocean for food. This was a lesson for the woman whose child would become, of course, Guruwul.

This is an old story. Older than everything. When the world was new, the lore was created, and the whale and the serpent looked about and saw the ocean.

I will look after the land because that is my home, but who will look after the ocean? said the serpent.

I will look after all the salt water, said the whale, because the fish and the turtles, the crabs and the weeds, the coral and the caves all need care.

But you will need to return to the land every now and then, said the serpent, to bring back your lore.

I will, said the whale. I will beach myself on the sand, I will come back to the land to regurgitate the lore so that the lore can be complete and the land and sea can know each other.

And that's how it has always been: the whale patrols the oceans and the serpent slides across the land, creating rivers and mountains, lakes and plains.

The dedication of the whale in regurgitating the lore is visible in the deep south of the world, where her many lives can be seen in a long row of her bones – thousands of bones, thousands of skeletons – counting the aeons of the earth. Those aeons are remembered in the lore, as the lore is observed.

One day the people saw a great cloud sail down the coast, following the path of the whale. *What is that cloud?* thought the serpent. The people were concerned and called on the serpent to tell them what to do. Watch that cloud, replied the serpent. So the people lit fires from headland to headland, all along the coast. At each point the cloud passed, fires sprang up and the smoke told the people in the south that a great cloud was approaching them.

An old man paddled a boat out to the island with no name so he could see the cloud more clearly. The old man had to ask permission of the whale and the serpent to visit the island because it was the island of boys' blood and men's scars. A sacred place only visited at the time of boy's blood and men's scars. He watched and he saw the ribs and the rigging. It is not a cloud, the old man decided; it is a giant pelican.

He paddled back to the land and told the people that the cloud was in fact a giant pelican and they must follow the pelican. I saw it from that island, he said, pointing to the east. The island with no name, he said. Barrangooba, that land is the land of the passing pelican.

Long after that pelican had passed, long after the people saw white people climb from the pelican's back, the man from the cave visited the island of the passing pelican with his son and other young men. They made their knives from a stone from the sea. They ate lobsters and shellfish as a spirit man instructed them in their ordeal. Each day the men and boys dived into the sea for the lobsters, and they laughed because the sea was warm and the reef was safe, but in the backs of their minds were the stone knives wrapped in the cloth of *kinny aha,* the leaf marked by the serpent's head.

Every morning, an hour before grandfather lifted his golden head from the sea, they heard the wolves of the sea. *Kwyy, wiii, yowroo,* cried the spirit birds. The men and boys listened, their heads still resting on their rolled-up clothes, within which they had hidden their blades.

Tomorrow, said the old man to the boys and the men and the man from the cave, tomorrow we will visit the whale and the shark. Do you have something for me?

The men and the boys felt for the knot of their narguns that tied their stone to them and they nodded. Yes, we have something for you.

Next morning, long before dawn, at the time when the wolves of the sea cried *kwyy, wii, yawoo* and the men and boys shuddered because the air from the sea was as cold as a snake's tooth and was full of the sounds of wolves, they huddled in the heath and waited. From the corners of their eyes they saw the old man lead the man from the cave away, and they waited. They saw the light of bird blood leak onto the very margin of the sky until one by one they were asked to contribute their colour to the rising sun, and that's when they saw looming above them the giant shark and the gigantic whale, and they stared between the two great figures and for the first time they realised that they had joined the contest of the deep sea.

One day they would be asked to observe the passage of the whale, witness her sacrifice, witness her escape from the shark, follow the journey of the whale to a point where all the land ends. There they would be told how nothing they do will match the dedication of the whale and the serpent, because that is the lore and they are mere followers of the lore. They did not invent it and they cannot destroy it. For the lore is not about success or failure, greed or power. It is about the land and the sea and our role in its continuance. The whale swims, the serpent coils: that is all.

EMBRASURE

EMBRASURE

She couldn't remember seeing a tree.

Even though every stone and gate, window and tile, could be raised in her mind as clearly as a brother or a sister's face.

Eighteen years she'd lived in Rosecastle Street, until the man had come and taken her away, and now, although she could see the uneven stitches trimming the coarse ruche to her mother's apron as clear as the veins in the back of her hand, she couldn't remember a tree. Along the whole length of Rosecastle Street and even Hedley Road, not one. She roamed the streets of the old town in her mind, turning down this lane and that until, yes, the common, the three elms in the common, the three trees of her entire life until now.

Oh, she'd read about trees, and tigers, ostriches, elephants, pyramids; everyone had in those days, they featured in the sentences on every blackboard, the exotic, the enthralling. That's how they got you to read. Even the daughters of coal miners. Everyone was a coal miner or a coal miner's wife or daughter, everyone. No, she couldn't remember a tree or any man who wasn't a coal miner. Except perhaps Edward Carmody at the shop ... and Father Williams the priest ... and old Fitzgerald at the school, but he died.

And now there was this man. He should have been a coal miner, but he'd come into her street one day and said he didn't intend to be a coal miner, no, he was going to be a landowner, on the other side of the world. She presumed he meant Africa and thought of monkeys and elephants in the garden, elephants cleverly spurting water onto the flowerbeds. There was a story like that in their reader, and she never wondered why the elephant didn't eat the flowers or tread on them. All the children, it seemed, had believed the story about the elephant.

And then this man came along and said to hell with the coal mine and she'd said to hell with Rosecastle Street and so here they were.

She watched his back. It was nothing to see a man with his shirt off in this country – often it was too hot otherwise, especially with the work they had to do. At first she'd blushed fiercely and turned away from any half-naked farmer or builder's boy, but gradually she'd learnt about backs.

And this back. She knew this back. Knew how the muscles corded beside the spine, plaited and stiff, like salted rope. She'd run her hands along those ropes and feel him squirm, run her thumb around the blade of the shoulder, along the collarbone, into the cavity of the neck, and let her fingers drift across his lips, find them wetted by the tip of his tongue, and then that was it – his back arched and he swung around and grabbed her by the waist, lifted her and brought her down on him. Naked and brown. You could do that in this country. No one to look in the window, no one to tell your mother, no one to see it as wrong.

Tonk. The mallet struck the wedge into the cleft log and the sound echoed off the trunks of red gum and wilga by the river. *Tonk,* he struck, and *tonk* again, the wedge popping the log, springing a fence post clean away from the timber, hard and solid and yet moistly pink, like a filleted salmon.

She looked across to where Violet was lying on her back in the cane basket, arms behind her head, legs splayed, boneless as a tulip. Just a nappy on. You could do that here. Not in summer, but in autumn – what they called autumn. In the dappled light beneath the tree, the tree she'd begged him to spare, her baby slept naked and tea-coloured, not at all like the babies at home, who all looked like unhealthy whey.

With the red dog asleep on the step, those little birds had come to creep among the twigs and leaves, piping to one another so quietly you could miss it if you didn't listen, not at all like the sparrows of Rosecastle Street. These were timid birds, secretive, innocent things, finnicking with insects so small they were invisible to her. And not at all like the red-and-blue lorikeets, whose military plumage and three-note bell songs seemed to promise a complete tune, but perhaps they only needed to remind one another of the opening bars so they could return to slicing gumnuts with their pincer bills, dropping the fragments, astringent and lemony, all around her. And on the baby once or twice, so that she made a mew with her tiny bright lips but returned to sleep without opening an eye or disturbing her dream of milk and warm-pressed breasts. You could do that in this country.

When she brought him a couple of scones and a cup of tea he drank it standing, keen to get on with his work. She slid her hand across the tight curve of his waist and a finger between the top of his trousers and his skin, let it slide into the hollow of his groin to feel his body tighten, his eyes flaring at her like a horse's and she,

she shimmied at him. What would her mother have said if she'd seen that sliding finger, the shameless shimmy? But there was no one to see, no one to say it was wrong.

He drew her to him and showed her how he was going to plane the flitches of timber to make the frames and shutters for their windows, and then he whispered a promise into her ear, so hot it burnt her cheeks. But you could do that in this country.

He was clever. She watched as he put a bevel on opposite corners of the timber, planing the sweet scrolls of wood from the plank so that the air became heady with eucalyptus. Without a word he held two pieces together at a right angle, looking up at her to see if she understood how they worked, that the bevel would set the frame out at an angle from the stone and make a slightly flared aperture. Do you see what this allows, his eyes seemed to ask.

All day he worked like that, and before the afternoon had passed he had framed up the two tall and narrow windows and fitted shutters to the other two. He'd cut the shutter timbers with a small notch so that, when brought together, they formed a heart just like those in a Swiss village she'd seen on the tins of the Wasser biscuits her mother used to buy at Christmas.

She stood back and admired the completeness, the neatness they leant to the front of the house, her house. But the sun was getting low now, almost below the crowns of the great trees by the river, and so he'd taken the red dog and brought up the flock of sheep, and the cows with their calves at foot, and penned them in the yard beside the shed. She'd already pitched in forkfuls of the sweet wild hay they'd cut from the riverbank their first summer here. And they looked at each other then with the first hint of uncertainty either had felt that day.

Magpies and kookaburras watching from the trees seemed to accept the yarding as the cue to roll out their impossibly wild and heedless songs, ending the day with bawdy riot, flagrant pipers of a contemptuous army.

The shutters brought darkness to the house earlier than before, so they lit lamps and polished chimney glass even before dusk had purpled the valley. She turned her back as he took the gun from the shelf and set it by the narrow aperture he'd fitted earlier, the timber still oozing with sweaty sap.

They prayed perfunctorily over their plates and looked up at each other briefly before dropping their gaze to the meal. She'd braised chunks of lamb, such big chunks she felt shame lest her mother find how profligate they'd become. Her own onions and carrots thickened the sauce, a chutney from the tomatoes that had sprung up of their own accord beside the pig's sty. A stack of bread and butter that threatened to topple from the plate. But you had to feed the man, he'd laboured from before dawn with barely a moment's rest, for they were hurrying, preparing the house.

They lay in bed, naked but for the sheet, and held to each other, she with an arm crooking his neck and the other straddling his back, and he likewise, except that one hand cupped her breast, the nipple standing out between his fingers fat and proud, dimpled, gauzy with its own dew. But they were listening.

Violet's breath was regular and sweet. No catch of croup or congestion, no muffled splutter from bedclothes too close. She, like them, could do with just a sheet, sleep resplendent with tossed limbs. You could do that here.

They weren't listening for her breath; they'd come to expect its unbroken regularity. But still they listened.

He settled himself so he could look across her shoulder at the dog, and when it lifted its muzzle, ears slowly pricking, he slid his arms from his wife, and crept from the bed to the tall window slot and levelled the gun through its aperture.

A cow coughed, a sheep gave a bleat, and they could hear the stamp of her defiant foot, the one the others saw as their leader. Again she stamped, bravely facing whatever there was to face, her yellow eyes swivelling about the moonlit yard, knowing but not seeing. And then the gun blasted silence from the blades of leaves, tore it from the mouths of sheep, caused cows to duck their heads to their calves, troubled, knowing but not seeing. Again the blast of the gun, and again. Not another noise. The moonlight resuming its delicate silvering of leaf edge, shovel blade, cheekbone and air.

She lay in bed staring towards the man at the window, Violet sucking at her breast, surprised to find herself in her mother's arms. What did they want, these people? Why did they keep coming back? Couldn't these people see they meant no harm, that all they wanted was to run a few sheep and cows, enough to raise their child – well, children soon, if she knew what was happening inside her.

He stood by the window, the gun arcing back and forth, the fortification allowing him to cover most of the yard. The particularity of the embrasure's angle a witness to their consternation, their fear, their knowledge that not all agreed with their claim.

Why didn't they leave him alone? Unconsciously he rested the fingers of one hand on the frame before becoming aware of the workmanship in it, the pride he'd invested in its construction. It was his: his window, his house. He'd made them and he'd keep them. He meant no harm to anyone, so why didn't they leave him alone?

All night he stood by the window, occasionally resting his weight on one leg, easing the tension in the muscles of the other, his forehead against the sweet timber, mouthing thanks that he'd got the job finished, windows shuttered, door secure, and the embrasure built from which to defend his right.

FRANKS IS DEAD

Everybody agrees that this is what happened: Franks and Flinders were killed by blows from steel hatchets landing so heavily that Franks' skull was driven into the turf. And that's the point at which agreement stops.

The *Champion* arrives at Point Gellibrand in Port Phillip Bay in 1836. On the ship Charles Franks has brought 500 sheep and a partner, George Smith, and a shepherd called either Flinders or Hindes, but nobody seems certain.

The waters off Point Gellibrand are shallow, clear and calm, crowded with mussels, oysters, flounder, flathead and garfish. Only twelve months earlier, Bunurong, Wathaurong and Woiwurrung people feasted on this bay of plenty; their ovens and houses are evident but already the people are scarce, avoiding the frenetic activity of the white people.

It is winter, but even so the days can be brilliant with mild sunshine, the wavelets scattering light as if from a shattered mirror. It is God's own country. A man might become anything here. In those days women could please themselves.

In this mood of limitless opportunity Franks removes his sheep from the *Champion* on 23 June and, on the advice of George

MacKillop, decides to take up land around Mount Cotterell, on the headwaters of the Barwon River. It takes until 2 July to cover the 20 miles (32 kilometres) of flat volcanic grasslands. After depasturing the sheep, George Smith returns to Point Gellibrand to bring up more stores.

On 8 July Smith arrives at Mount Cotterell. He sees no sign of Franks or Flinders but the stores appear to have been ransacked.

He takes fright and returns to Point Gellibrand, where he conscripts the help of Mr Malcolm, Mr Clark, Mr George Sams, Mr Armytage, Dr Barry Cotter, Charles Wedge and Mr Gellibrand. Gellibrand asks Henry Batman to accompany him, with William Windberry, George Hollins, Michael Leonard, Benbow, Bullett, Stewart and Joe the Marine. On the way they fall in with Mr Wood and his large party, which includes David Pitcairn, Mr Guy, Derrymock, Baitlange, Ballyan and Mr Alexander Thomson.

So, a party of well over twenty-three people are curious enough to drop what they are doing to investigate the upsetting of a cask of flour at Mount Cotterell. Or have they already mounted similar expeditionary forces since the establishment of the first Yarra settlement less than a year before? Are they at war with the Kulin Nation and recognise this as a beachhead in the battle for possession of the Port Phillip plains? When Captain William Lonsdale is appointed police magistrate of Port Phillip in July 1836, the frontier community is under token jurisdiction, but it is an indelible indication of the true activities of the previous twelve months that when George Smith notices an upturned barrel of flour he has no trouble in mobilising a small army to investigate the cause.

These men, who do not believe a delinquent possum is rampant, mount a force of heavily armed volunteers. They are not involved in casual reprisal but a calculated vigilante campaign. The party follows a trail of flour and discarded stores and comes across a band of about seventy to one hundred Wathaurong people. In responding to Lonsdale's investigation of the incident, Henry Batman says he yelled at them but they didn't move so he fired his gun once above their heads and they ran; John Wood says several shots were fired but none could have caused death because they were fired from too great a distance; Edward Wedge believes that the nature of the cuts to the heads of Franks and Flinders, whose bodies were found near the stores, indicates infliction 'with a particular type of long-handled hatchet' that he gave to the natives earlier in the year 'to conciliate them'; Michael Leonard says several shots were fired but to his knowledge no one was injured; William Windberry says that the party went after the blacks to retrieve the stolen property but he does not think any were killed.

William Lonsdale receives the evidence and advises the colonial secretary that no harm has been inflicted on the Aboriginal people despite it being common knowledge in the colony that at least twelve have been killed. The Wathaurong say over thirty-five but, of course, they are never invited to give evidence. No investigation is made of other attacks that follow the first punitive expedition.

The court hears that the murderers of Franks and Flinders are Goulburn Aboriginals Dumdom and Callen. The Daugwurrung are the people of the Goulburn River, and this evidence places them in Wathaurong and Woiwurrung country, but given known clan movements of the time this is unlikely. But to the avengers, one group of Aborigines is much the same as any other.

George Smith says it is impossible that Charles Franks could have provoked the murder because he 'had a great aversion to the native blacks, and would not give them food, thinking it the best way to prevent them from frequenting the station'. He arrived for the first time only days before at a 'station' at the headwaters of the Barwon River, heartland of the Wathaurong and Woiwurrung people, a land they would defend with their lives.

Mr Franks is 'very mild and gentle in his general conduct, and I do not think he would molest anyone', concludes his partner, Mr Smith, but Robert William von Stieglitz, in a letter to his brother, casts a different light on Franks' gentle demeanour. Stieglitz went to Franks to buy lead, which all knew Franks had in great supply. Franks told Stieglitz that the lead was excellent for 'making blue pills for the natives'. Some historians take the word 'pill' literally and assume it is a euphemism for the manufacture of strychnine to lace bullock carcasses in order to poison Aborigines, a common practice in the colony and further refined in Port Phillip. When challenged about this practice, it was a common defence to say that the poison had been for the crows. This was a popular jest in Port Phillip because at the time many referred to the blacks by the American euphemism 'Jim Crow'. It's more likely, however, that Franks was making his own shotgun balls.

Either way, it seems this mild-mannered Christian was murdering Aborigines to secure the 'selection' he and his partners, George Smith and George Armytage, had decided upon. It seems he came upon his 'great aversion to the blacks' in a very short space of time, perhaps even in advance of meeting them, so that he thought it necessary to bring the ingredients of their destruction in his first stores.

Joseph Tice Gellibrand, who until recently was the attorney-general of Tasmania, and is now the token representative of law and order for the Port Phillip Association, writes of the Franks murder on 7 August 1836: 'Several parties are now after the natives and I have no doubt many will be shot and a stop put to this system of killing for bread.' The press are also phlegmatic in their understanding of the true nature of the conflict. *The Cornwall Chronicle* records the event thus: 'The avenging party fell on the guilty tribe ... and succeeded in annihilating them.'

It's only twelve months since the arrival of the colonists and yet it is a matter of conversation, among men meeting for the first time, how to eliminate the annoying insistence of the indigenes to protect their land.

Entrepreneurs in Van Diemen's Land, frustrated by the restrictions being placed on land acquisition, determine to form a company to take up the green fields discovered by sealers at Port Phillip. In their correspondence they discuss the advantages of taking up broad acres where no civil authority exists to hamper their enterprise. Mindful of the colonial administration's increasing desire to ameliorate the indigenes and the Van Diemen's Land governor's determination to uphold that line, they confect a series of documents to disguise the true nature of their activities. The clans of the Kulin peoples surrounding Port Phillip and Western Port are about to experience one of the most blatant thefts in the history of humankind.

John Batman and John Pascoe Fawkner are both sons of convicts and have built fortunes from property in Van Diemen's Land. They join forces to become the two principals of the Port Phillip Association. Batman is a chaotic character, and his nature swings erratically between acts of kindness and bloody-minded self-interest, while Fawkner is a more calculating and meticulous

personality. Within days of landing at Port Phillip they are at logger-
heads, Batman parading around the settlement with Aborigines he
has brought from Sydney, and Fawkner making plans for hotels and
newspapers, the stuff of prosperous settlements. But their different
humours don't prevent them from cooperating in the wholesale
division of the Kulin lands.

Some of the most astute businessmen in Hobart helped establish the Port Phillip Association, and they are joined by the more
entrepreneurial members of the administration and judiciary. It is
a formidable combination of law and enterprise: the entrepreneurs
providing cash and energy and the legal minds steering the association through the administrative shoals of colonial government by
concocting sham documents of possession in the most portentous
and arcane language.

These men are involved in very influential circles, and know
how to weasel their way around Governor Arthur's instructions.
Batman, Fawkner, Gellibrand, Charles Swanston and others are
the most celebrated businessmen in the colony, and their plot to
gazump the authorities and the real owners of the land is still celebrated in Australia today as the bringing of the light to the heathen
wasteland instead of the white-shoe-brigade land sham it really was.

Thousands of pounds change hands in weeks as frantic entrepreneurs throw themselves at the association in their haste to secure
land. Most land is 'selected' unsurveyed and thousands of sheep
are offloaded on the tranquil shores of Point Gellibrand, where as
many as eight ships ride at anchor on any given day, such is the
speed of 'settlement'. In fact, some of the party sent to revenge
Franks' murder are recruited from the crew and passengers of
these ships.

Nothing happens at random here; this is an orchestrated campaign where the colonists work against both the Kulin Nation and the colonial governments in Sydney and Hobart.

The unanimity of the colonists' purpose can be gauged by their relationships with one another. They are eager to see all the lands populated by like-minded individuals to thwart the government's purposes, and to murder and disperse the black population to secure the 'peace'. Indeed, they go to great lengths to ensure that their friends join the colony, their letters confirming that they are anxious to create a solid confederacy to protect their interests and obscure the deceits instituted to acquire them.

George MacKillop, who admires Smith, Armytage and Franks in their precipitous lust for land, is experienced in the process of dispossession, having already applied the procedure to great effect in India, where he worked in partnership with Charles Swanston. Swanston would go on to become exceedingly rich in Port Phillip, his interests in land and banking making him one of its most respected and powerful citizens. Swanston and MacKillop have extensive business dealings with the staunch churchman George Smith, Franks' fellow squatter. These are respectable people, already wealthy from their Indian and Van Diemen's Land investments, churchgoers, solid citizens, good enough to name streets after, but they are directly involved in the war to dispossess the Kulin people. How do these solid citizens justify their actions?

They describe the murder of the 'gentle' Franks as an 'outrage', the term coined for the action of a black man raising a hand against a white, not patriots desperate to protect their lands, but criminals to be destroyed before justice can intervene. They urge other settlers to 'full satisfaction' against the blacks. Black resistance is labelled criminality, for to equate it with armed resistance is to acknowledge prior ownership.

The squatters applaud the appointment of the police magistrate Foster Fyans in Geelong. Fyans has earned the sobriquet 'Flogger' for his administration of 'justice' at Moreton Bay and Norfolk Island, and the esteem with which the gentlemen of Port Phillip regard him has been earned by his thoroughness in defending their lands in the Indian colonial war.

What is establishing itself in Port Phillip is a close-knit club of men experienced in dispossession, war, treachery and silence, their experience gained in the British Empire's most recent wars against legitimate landowners. This is a land war, and it is conducted in the same manner as any other in the history of conflict between nations.

At Portland, to the west of Port Phillip, the Henty brothers have already established a sealing colony, and the conflict with the Gunditjmara people is symbolised by a clash on the beach for possession of a single whale. Both sides probably see it as a beach head in the fight for possession of the soil itself. The battle site becomes known as the Convincing Ground, the place where the Gunditjmara are 'convinced' of white rights to the land. The Gunditjmara are beaten in that battle but never convinced of its legitimacy. Today we continue to act as if the Aboriginal warriors are criminals rather than people defending the land from infidels.

PEACEABLE KINGDOM

J ust sixteen years of exposure to Christianity and my intellectual curiosity was snuffed.

I realised this last week when I arrived for work in a strange capital and to stranger accommodation. I was unsurprised by the weird décor, but too tired to talk to the people I was supposed to meet and too awake to sleep. So I read the walls.

The art displayed in motels, hotels, corrugated-iron red-desert demountables, the prim spare rooms of friends of the arts, and caravan parks holds a grim fascination that has replaced the hole left after my tentative faith finally took flight – presumably fleeing to a more willing audience at Hillsong, where it was certain to receive the full Mexican wave and swoon; the postures of certainty and the conviction of the chosen.

There were two old prints of animals and children in a style as familiar to my generation as the Hoover twin tub. The borders ran with a text I must have seen a thousand times in my life. You see it in people's homes, old wares shops, the maudlin manse, school halls and virtuous hospitals: *The wolf also shall dwell with the lamb, and the leopard shall lie down with the kid and the calf and the lion and the fatling together; and a little child shall lead them.*

Both pictures were similar and the texts almost identical. The art depicted benign lambs and leopards, innocent goats and a milk-fed, chubby child leading a dangerous animal. Even the cows looked like they'd never kicked over a bucket or thought of butting the dairyman. It was called the *Peaceable Kingdom of the Branch*.

The rest of the furniture was all old colonial bumf, so I read these texts with mild interest simply because there were no jam tins handy. And then I saw in the background what I'd never noticed before. In one print, almost hidden by a bridge, was a group of figures. I stood on the bed to get a closer look. Yes, I did take my boots off. I was paying, but I can't stand vandalism. I was brought up in a family where at least two aunts owned a variety of these same prints and despised children who stood on beds.

I had never finished reading these texts in the past because I could sniff out a biblical passage from ten metres and was intent on eluding the entrapments of the mild Christ and his devout follow-ers. When I visited my aunts as a teenager I was already protesting against the Vietnam War, where we were told we had God on our side, and fighter planes were embellished with the Christian cross. Or Marilyn Monroe. Both intrinsic to our cultural campaigns.

I had to peer at the texts because the faux Victorian lamps were mere decorations. Up close I could see that the tiny tableau beneath the bridge was dominated by men in tricorn hats who extended their hands in Christian kindness to a group almost bowed in devotion: Native Americans with feathers, skin tunics and awed, supplicant faces.

I went to the sister print and there was a similar scene. On the other side of a river from where the bouncing babe was leading a leopard, the tricorn hats were advising Native Americans of their good fortune. The text of this one began, *When the great Penn his famous treaty made with the Indian chiefs in the elm-trees shade, the wolf and all that other nonsense laid down with whomever.*

I stared at these prints for an hour, impaled as if by a butterfly collector's pin. This was the art and text of Christian colony. Every brushstroke, every word, had been calculated to appease the spirit. Not the spirits of the Native Americans – theirs were crushed within months of meeting the hats. It was the Christian spirit that needed a salve, a godly reason for taking another's land.

I leant against the wall, overwhelmed by the meticulous planning and implementation. The actual taking of the land was made possible by those vandals and goths, common in any society, who arrived on whaling boats and galleons. Their lust for women and gold had always made colonial transition so much easier. It was said the smallpox contagion was deliberately applied to blankets and given to resistant bands of indigenes: to infect, demoralise, depopulate and depress.

William Penn was a wealthy English Quaker who was given a tract of land that he called Pennsylvania. He arrived in 1681 determined to raise a community dedicated to the gentle words of the Sermon on the Mount. He was said to deal kindly with the Native Americans, for which they were grateful. Those on their knees are likely to be grateful for the extended hand of a gentle man. They granted Penn an extension of his land measured by an area that could be walked in a day and a half. Penn's successors cleared a path of trees and logs and trained athletes to run as far as they could in a day and a half. In relay. They claimed 1200 square miles of land.

It wasn't Penn's intention to claim so much, but his 'treaty' with the Native Americans could only be forged because the Native

Americans by 1684 had become impoverished and powerless. He couldn't be blamed for the actions of his descendants, but it says a lot about the ability of the Sermon on the Mount to saturate the Christian soul.

Those who wrought the relay ruse of land acquisition were now represented in this West Brisbane guesthouse by a chubby angelic child whose conquest of savage beasts, which quivered to nuzzle the child's plump paw, represented the conquest of the Americas by Christians. The savage spirit quelled and brought to heal by the mildest of restraint.

I stared and I stared. The elaborate performance and explanation of colony was deeply embedded in both the Bible and the Church, and we are lulled into believing the story by tracts as pervasive as the chubby child's personal circus. My aunts, attempting sanctity, had adorned their walls with similar prints, and at the same time condemned their ancestors' history, to be reworked by athletic coaches and the painters of pastel Sunday-school posters.

I stepped off the bed, put my boots on and walked into the balm of a Brisbane spring. I bought an Indian curry and naan and two frosty beers and returned to the verandah of the guesthouse to consume the meal while overlooking a darkening garden of palm and fern and fruit bat. As the beads of frost slipped down the flank of my Tasmanian beer, I considered myself. Me, the radical, the provocateur, the sage of history and cynicism, and I'd completely underestimated the calculated pervasion of the British colonial myth.

We'd been fed this pap of propaganda since our eyes could focus and our ears could recognise words. Many of us bore the names of famous Christians; the songs our mothers sang while baking apple pie were preparing us for our delusion. The mere presence of sacred babies lulled us into the complacency of acceptance.

Isaiah was preparing us for a Golden Age when snakes would not bite, lambs and lions would cuddle up and war would be no more. Lovely. In Job we read that 'you will have a covenant with the stones of the field, and the wild animals will be at peace with you'. Isaiah claimed, 'He will judge between the nations and will settle disputes for many peoples. They will beat their swords into plough-shares and their spears into pruning hooks. Nation will not take up sword against nation, nor will they train for war anymore.' Lovelier still; a sylvan paradise.

Ezekiel said, 'I will make a covenant of peace with them and rid the land of wild beasts so that they may live in the desert and sleep in the forests in safety.' So the Christian would compensate for God's bad halo days and rid the earth of dangerous beasts and tame the land. For Christians. The implication is clear. Penn cautioned his followers that there is only one God, and only Christians can expect to inhabit the Golden Age of peace and kindness. All others will be converted … or lost.

When Edward Hicks began his series of paintings on the subject of lambs and leopards, fatlings and innocence, he was painting from a deep Quaker belief, but at a time when he was disquieted by the failure of his fellow Quakers to live in harmony with one another.

Despite his concerns, however, he has interpreted the Bible correctly; it calls for man's dominion over all the wild beasts and places. Despite the presence of other peoples in those wild places, all Christians presumed that it was their duty to defeat nature and soothe the savage breast.

The curry was good, the beer was better, the night a balm of silk to the skin. But old misery guts chewed the rag of history.

Most of Australia's 'explorers' were devout Christians, but many experienced dark nights of the soul when hints of regret briefly illuminated their conscience. The Protector of Aborigines, George Augustus Robinson, was beguiled by the Indigenous night fishing fleets on the Murray River, and you can feel how tantalised he was by the word 'civilisation'. He resisted the allure successfully, but he was always conscious that the colonial presence was poisonous to the Indigenous population and had no intention of providing justice for them. His own ministrations, of course, he considered the actions of divine grace.

Thomas Mitchell rode through villages of more than 1000 Aboriginal people and envied the grace, comfort and individuality of their homes, but his admiration always succumbed to his assumption that this way of life had to give way to Christian industry. Mitchell observed fields of harvested grain, but it was months before he realised, or admitted in his diary, that this was an act of industry.

Charles Sturt was near death when his most blinding realisation of Aboriginal achievement furrowed his Christian brow. On top of a sand dune in the dead heart of Australia he was hailed by 400 Aborigines. He could barely make them out, such was the progress of his disease, but the horses staggered down the dune and Sturt was aware that if the Aborigines had aggressive intent his whole party was doomed.

Instead, the people brought coolamons of water to slake the thirst of the 'explorers', and then held out those coolamons gingerly to the horses, creatures they had never seen. The explorers were given food. Tubs of well water were set beside their accommodation. They were provided with kindling for their fire.

Lying on his bed that night, Sturt could see the winking fires of all the houses spread across the Warburton valley. He was enchanted by the laughter and singing as the little town prepared its meals. Women ground grain into flour and Sturt reported the charm of the soft whirring of the mills as if they were a fable of peace. The Golden Age. By ten o'clock the village was silent and at rest. It was an almost Christianly civility.

But Sturt was aware that any entreaty he might make on behalf of these people would fall on the ears of men who had not lain down with the lamb. How were those women to know that the whisk of their mills was an anthem of doom?

Hicks painted his Golden Age idylls and plucked verses from the Bible to declare the loveliness of the future for Christians.

I went back to my room, my mind running with these thoughts, took off my boots like my aunts would have me do, and stood on the bed to look at the paintings again. I didn't know Edward Hicks from a bar of soap, I did not know the verses had come from Isaiah, but I looked at the angle of the Christian hands and how the Native Americans meekly bent their necks and I knew that this was how we explained ourselves. Afterwards.

Did we really believe in a Golden Age, or were we happier to give its name to a hotel, utilising the heavy irony of the subeditors from *The Age* who drank there and fashioned within its walls one of the more debauched hotels of Melbourne?

I realised I was in no mood for the polite, ruminative laments on black fate by white writers, but at the appointed time, a time my parents and aunts adored, I walked down the hill through the hub of old West End. A woman, stiffened with multiple sclerosis and hectic with need, was begging for $7.50 to restore her mobile phone to credit. Blackfellas in doorways responded to a wave with one hand while cradling a bottle in the other. The Golden Age.

West End was being gentrified; these beggars and paupers would soon be evicted not only from their houses but also from the suburb. That's why it could now afford a refined bookshop, refined talk and tapas.

I tried to rally for the sisters who read their verse, and memoir, clapped the white ladies in their $500 dresses. There was not an unworthy word read nor an unkind thought in the courtyard of that benign bookshop. But the Branch bent above us all and dripped its sanctity in translucent pearls. Penn would have seen his mission vindicated, Hicks would have lifted his brush to one of the hundred versions he painted of the quieted beasts and the ring-leading child.

For whom is the Golden Age reserved? The athletic coaches who devised a ruse no better than that of the man who buys shares at half price from old people addled with oncoming dementia? The man who bought Melbourne for a handful of beads and promised goods that were never delivered?

Was there a time, or will there ever be such a time, when men will not be craven?

As I trudged up Boundary Street, I was allowed safe passage by the rap-hall patrons who stepped aside to avoid the spectre of one whose age they could not comprehend.

'I ain't gunna study war no more, I ain't gunna study war no more,' we sang in the seventies, pleased to have rescued the lyrics from 'Down by the Riverside', and convinced a song would lead us into the Golden Age. But the words are from the traditional Negro rendition of Isaiah's 'nor will they train for war anymore'.

Is it impossible for us to escape the Bible?

Back on the verandah with the bats and palms, I stared into the darkness, heavy with tropical perfumes and stitched by the stridulations of insects. War and faith, war and faith; the Bible was full of its contest, or the use of one to justify the other.

The tricorn hats in Hicks' paintings had only offered the kindly hand once the war was over and the treaty bargains had been made certain. My eye roamed over the lovely architectural features of the old timber guesthouse. Octagonal turrets had been constructed in three positions on the roof above the verandah to direct cooler draughts onto the deck. A trick learned in the colonies of India and America and repeated here in our version of colonial architecture to cool the heads of governors and million-acre graziers.

This grand old house had been one of the first mansions on this side of the Brisbane River and had housed an assortment of government officials and gentry. It was styled for those with languid grace. For years it had hosted dinners and balls for visiting British dignitaries, the machinery of colonialism – or as the Wiradjuri writer Jeanine Leane would have it, the British diaspora. You couldn't turn a corner of the many corridors without some artistic or textual reference to the Bible. This house had once been at the heart of Britain's triumphant victory over the savage.

The savage who milled grain in a susurration of stone against stone, the savage who sang and laughed at the end of the day, who could design a house to reflect her personality (Mitchell believed it was the women who made the design choices), who could dine on roast duck and cake, and sip cool well water in a place we have since named Sturt's Stony Desert.

A publishing house charged with the study of Aboriginal and Torres Strait Islander culture has been arguing with me for years about the existence of Aboriginal agricultural industries. Many of the accepted experts on Aboriginal history are spooked when the word 'agriculture' is used for acts that they have proclaimed, in their certainty, hunting and gathering. Bill Gammage's *The Biggest Estate* declares that Australia was a managed Aboriginal landscape and has been very well received, so perhaps we are becoming more curious, less reflexively panicked by questions about our historical assumptions.

Let's hope so, but those leather-patch professors were also driven to dyspepsia by my discussion of the absence of war in Aboriginal Australia. What about the nulla-nulla, they cried, what about the killer boomerang? But I wasn't talking about that grand old human predilection to murder, I was talking about land war, colonial war.

The stability of Australian first languages over 120,000 years is testament not only to diplomatic restraint but also to the trans-continental agreement to live on and protect portions of the land. Remaining so long on discrete districts allowed the continuance of over 350 individual languages. If land war erupted every forty to fifty years, as it had in Europe and Asia, smaller, weaker units would have been obliterated or absorbed, and their words gobbled by the dominant language.

If our grain harvesters, fish processors and fruit preservers had been charged with the custodianship of particular river systems and ranges, and their whirring mills had been sibilant every evening across the ages, the songs they sang at dawn and dusk would be rich with reference to their preserve, and the language would become a reflection of the environment.

Any student of Aboriginal languages will become aware, as the speakers have always been, that each language has a distinct sound and intonation. It might resemble sister languages strung along the culturelines like beads on a necklace, but it remains distinct because of the land on which the speakers dwell and for which no other people have the same depth of knowledge or responsibility.

Was that the Golden Age? Can it be the template for a new Golden Age? Responsibility for the land, not ownership of it or the wealth it can generate?

Oh, Eddie Hicks, I love your oxen, I think your lambs are the cuddliest little moccasins I've ever seen, your chubby child could surely sell Snugglers nappies today. It would be nice if the vipers didn't bite and the leopard never stalked; but that's how your God made them, Eddie. I'd love to talk to you about this because the final word of any Christian I've discussed Creation with is that when in doubt you must have faith. I had faith in Andrew Johns, the disgraced rugby player; I had faith that Jim Cassidy just rode horses, not organised their performances with Tony Mokbel. I never had faith in Lance Armstrong but was asked to by beneficiaries of his charity. I was told to have faith and ignore the paedophile church leaders. I don't have a good record with faith.

I can't see the harm in someone believing in Mohammad, someone else in Christ, another in the sanctity of cows, another in the spiritual efficacy of the sun, yet another in a little boy numerically designated as the Holy One, but when a disciple decides that one god is sillier than his own and therefore another must cede his land and life, that's when faith deserts.

If our religions insisted on adherence to gentle codes of behaviour and observance, we might live longer and better. The incorporation of the mysteries of the universe and life into earthly existence is one thing; to exclude and punish those whose explanation of those mysteries is fractionally different is another. And to use those explanations as an excuse to steal is a simple, transparent and abominable device.

I am fascinated by faith. I once had the immense and accidental good fortune to be on the same train as Fred Chaney, ex-parliamentarian and former deputy leader of the Australian Liberal Party, as we travelled to visit the art galleries of Rome and Milan. Fred is a Christian intellectual. He dashed from one iconic work to the next, sharing the history of each in vivid detail. His enthusiasm for his culture was entrancing, his quiet love for his family an inspiration.

Those couple of days taught me a lot about history and goodness, but did not loosen one brick of my faith in country. Later, wandering around a Byzantine church on Torcello, Venice, my new knowledge reinforced my belief that the Eurasian religious habit of war, rape and pillage could not justify the rich objects of its culture. A belief that requires the severing of babies' heads and the slicing of unborn infants from wombs by the righteous sword encourages not just bigotry and violence but also disregard for the humanity of others.

The commercial and political ethics that produced Nazi Germany, Pol Pot's Cambodia and the global financial crisis are all excused in the minds of the perpetrators by their right to despise others for tiny differences, or simply justified by the opportunity to inflict harm. Fragments of that intolerance can be seen in the paybacks and punishments of Aboriginal Australia, but the restraint on these traits, which are so common to the human spirit, is the land itself. Traditional, pre-colonial Aboriginal faith is embedded in the land, and the responsibility for a particular district prevents all but the most fleeting outbreaks of violence. Soon the land calls back those it has created to observe the necessary functions of custodianship: that particular piece of land and no other.

If in all human societies there is another more likely to survive a few thousand years, it seems unknown to history or faith. I'm biased, but I yearn for that Golden Age where people stayed at home and harvested their grain in peace. And sang at dusk as they turned the bounty into cake. Artists paint those scenes today, venerating the peaceable land, but unlike Edward Hicks, they don't need to paint a hidden miniature beneath a bridge or branch to explain how they came to own the land of others.

That's why I stood on the bed for so long; I was lost in wonder. Not certainty, but the calm security of doubt. Wonder is the mainspring of hope and justice, and certainty is the excuse for its murder.

DEAR JOHN

Dear John,

There is nothing like being Australian.

We take for granted that we'll be able to fill up the car with petrol and go where we like. Few are so poor that they can't enjoy the privilege of unfettered travel and a good meal at the end of the day. We are fortunate to have a parliamentary democracy, despite your wilful insult to its integrity. We are lucky to have such a climate, such bountiful produce, such a small population. If the mood takes us we can tow a tinpot caravan right around the country and pull up every night in a caravan park with a sea view at sunset.

We rarely worry about being mugged, bombed or hungry. We took your advice and became relaxed, comfortable and alert. But never alarmed.

Apart from one section of our population, the mortality rate of our children is among the lowest in the world. Most of us believe we'll see our children grow up to be happy and wealthy.

If the country had to be colonised – and that was inevitable – you could do worse than the British. The institutions in this country work on the assumption that they are there to serve the people, even though that assumption is being sorely eroded by the parliamentarians of both major parties. I bet you pray for Kim every night, John; it's like having a gullible brother, isn't it? Iraq, detention, blackfellas – you think like Siamese twins, don't you?

John, you worship the inheritance of British colonial government, but everything else this country counts as its fortune comes from the land itself, including a democratic and egalitarian inclination. You weren't big on Aboriginal studies as a boy, but if you'd got your nose out of Wisden for a few minutes you would have been surprised about how democratic Aboriginal society really was. If your mate George W. read about a people who made decisions in a council of Elders, where everybody's right to food and shelter was enshrined, where each person's participation in society was unfettered, he'd probably boom, 'Hey, Donald, don't bomb those people, they must be Americans.' But you bomb them every day, John. I can see you enjoy it.

Our Australia today is a wealthy place. Few Australians would choose to live anywhere else, particularly places your mate George doesn't like. But we must never take our country for granted or stand by while an equal opportunity is withheld from any of our countrymen and women. Examples of how our silence damages our democracy are as frequent and as recent as yesterday.

You don't know Robert Lowe, John; he's black. Robert is an Aboriginal Elder from Warrnambool and tells a story that never fails to shock me. In a yarn about his boyhood he casually remarks that the Gunditjmara of Warrnambool were never allowed to enter the main commercial precinct of the town.

The year was 1973. Aboriginal kids were prevented from mixing in the streets with white people. Gough Whitlam was in power, pouring sand into the hands of the Gurindji and bringing the troops home from Vietnam. In the same decade, people demonstrated against the visit of the South African Springbok rugby team and cheered Nelson Mandela, but black people couldn't walk the streets of Warrnambool.

Aboriginal people from New South Wales and Western Australia have shown me the tickets that were handed out by government to allow them to enter a hotel or drive a car. Blackfella in a car? Must be stolen. Blackfella in a pub? Must be drunk.

This is recent Australian history, John, *this* is our heritage.

But there is never time or excuse for despair because the majority of Australians do not believe in treating people unequally; most believe racism to be anathema. Despairing leftists tell me not to be so gullible and point to the last three federal elections, but elections don't just test one belief or need, they record the population's sentiment across a range of concerns. One of those concerns is always self-interest, sometimes greed, but more often than not governments are elected after scaring the people to death or crippling their natural scepticism. Most people have others to support, and few of us would remain immune to falls in income or sudden unemployment. A cunning politician will make this fear the central plank of his election strategy; few have risked the dangerous proposal of stiffening the country's moral spine. Ring a bell, John?

While the left bemoans its fate and blames the electorate, Robert Manne urges people to defy the politicians and act on the better part of our soul. Manne is right; there is no time for either despair or blame. Michael Long, the former AFL footballer from Essendon, hasn't given up hope. Despite a famous letter to you expressing anger at your refusal to acknowledge the Stolen Generations, Long walked to Canberra in December 2004 in an attempt to plead the cause of justice. He wanted to draw your attention to Aboriginal issues, including the damage caused to the families of the Stolen Generations, a fate both his parents suffered. You refused to meet him until one of your Victorian minders reminded you who Michael Long was: a sportsman!

Warren Mundine is one of the few national Aboriginal spokespeople to have accepted a position on your National Indigenous Council. Long, Noel Pearson, Mick Dodson, Pat Dodson and Paul Briggs rejected the proposal. Those who accept are responsible, successful people, but most are from the business or the sporting worlds; too few have held political positions within their community. Mundine proposes that Native Title legislation be abandoned in favour of cash payments to communities to kick-start Indigenous enterprises. There is merit in enabling direct involvement of Aboriginal and Torres Strait Islander people in the economy, but as Mick Dodson said in December 2004, 'perhaps Mr Mundine doesn't understand what *land* means to Indigenous people'.

I know you would love to implement a policy to eliminate one of the last identifying characteristics of Aboriginal and Torres Strait Islander people because it would allow your government to treat everybody *equally*. That is, to merge everybody into one culture: white culture.

You take a clinical approach to Aboriginal and Torres Strait Islander issues, John, because you know most Australians skipped Australian history too. *Sir, we've already done Aborigines*. My oath you have, John. You say, We've spent millions on them, what are they whingeing about? Some of the Stolen Generations (although you'd never use the label) had better lives than if they'd stayed in camp with alcohol-dependent parents, what's the problem?

Well, John, the problem is that most of the children involved were taken against the wishes of their parents, did not have better lives or educations, and the damage is still sending shockwaves through the population. One woman I know cannot celebrate Mother's Day or Christmas because it recalls the misery of a child locked in an institution throughout the years when children should be with their mothers and looking forward with hopeful anticipation to Christmas.

In most Aboriginal communities there is not one family unaffected by this issue, John. It is serious. It can be fixed – you don't have to say sorry, you needn't use the word 'stolen' if you don't like, but we just want you to read a little history, and try someone other than Geoffrey Blainey. Blainey is a gentle and conscientious man, but he is only one man with one opinion, and he's snow-blind. Did you read the recommendations of the Royal Commission into Aboriginal Deaths in Custody? Of course you did, so you'll have read the heartbreaking testimony of hundreds of mothers who had their children taken from them and who spent the rest of their lives looking for those children and were met with cynical and obstructive interference from most churches and government departments.

John, I know you think that the problems besetting the Aboriginal and Torres Strait Islander community are our own fault, that if we got jobs, stopped drinking, stopped bludging, became just like other Australians, we wouldn't have anything to whinge about. But John, just a few facts that haven't been included in the *ABC Cricket Book*: the appalling levels of health standards in the Aboriginal community are not due to indigeneity; they are shared by the poor in any country on earth. Changing the belief or skin colour of these people will not solve these problems. The only thing that can restore the living standards of Aboriginal people is equity in the land over which they were once sovereign.

You made people fear for their clothesline and barbeque in your campaign to thwart the court's decision to acknowledge the fact of that sovereignty, John, but I know you don't believe that's what *Wik* meant. You've read the court's decision, you've read the Native Title legislation, you knew private land could not be compromised by these decisions, but you knew the heart of your people well, John, you knew they wouldn't mind if you told them that, gave them a reason to kick the black bastards in the behind.

It seems other facts have eluded the entire parliament too, John. Did you know that the greatest attendance at Christian churches is by Aborigines? Did you know that the most abstemious Australians, those most likely to be teetotallers, apart from Muslims, are Aborigines? Did you know that the highest birth rate in Australia is in the Aboriginal community? Not only are most blackfellas righteous and sober, but there's going to be more of them, too.

Do you really think you'd lose an election if you read those pages from the Bureau of Statistics 1998 census report on Alan Jones' radio program? Or are you happy for Australians to continue to believe what they believe? Do you share the opinion of our first two prime ministers on the relative value of the colours black and white? You know, John, I don't think it would cost the nation one dollar to acknowledge how the country began. There'd still be a Boxing Day Test, mates would still stand around their barbeques having a few coldies, the economy would still function, waves would still break at Bondi. The only difference would be that if a black Australian turned up in the backyard and grabbed a frosty can from the esky, the conversation wouldn't fall deathly silent; we'd be able to tell each other yarns about our family, enjoy the jokes about Gillespie's hair ... Oh, sorry John, he's a blackfella too. Well, Lehmann then, how he lost the race against Richardson to prove he was the slowest cricketer on earth ... Oh, but we can't talk about that either because he thinks Sri Lankans are black c***s, yelled it on television. Is there nothing we can all talk about together?

That's all we're on about, John, basic decency. We can work together and we'll make a stronger not weaker country as a result, but first we need to know the same things about the past. We know that there is much that frustrates you about Aboriginal affairs – it frustrates us too – but we want you to know our history and your part in it, and relying on the education you received at school will not tell you how we experienced the last 230 years. Most Aboriginal people don't want money from the government, would simply settle for acknowledgement of their history. Further justice would flow automatically and naturally from that knowledge and cost much less than the failed foreign currency trade of Treasurer Peter Costello. Oh, but you don't want to talk about that either, I suppose.

You pride yourself on being a *reasonable* man, and Aboriginal and Torres Strait Islander people see acknowledgement of demonstrable Indigenous history as a *reasonable* expectation. Keith Windshuttle can argue about how many deaths make a massacre or how many battles make a war, but he's yelling into a kerosene tin, all boom and echo. Arguments of the quantitative right need not stand in the way of good policies that will enhance the lives of all Australians. We can all reap economic, moral and psychological benefit from just policies that recognise the entire history of the land.

This is not what I was thinking on 9 October 2004. There were bleaker thoughts in my head, but then I turned to the land and it took me in its arms, as it always does. Most Australians might find it acutely embarrassing to talk about falling into the land's embrace, but it is our one true and lasting solace. The farax we eat as children comes from that land, our mother's milk springs from it, and the last thing to enter our mouths will be the soil of our graves. It will be important for us to have earnt that soil's respect and love.

Anyway, after the election fish still swam in the river. John Who, Alexander What, they asked dreamily. Azure kingfishers still flew like blue neon darts along the bank. The mussels had not fled to more egalitarian seas. On a sandbar baby stingrays were testing submerged flight in such studied, laborious strokes that I was awed by their innocent vulnerability to the sea eagles – creatures much more moved by the sight of unprotected flesh than by inherent beauty and naked hope.

I climbed a ridge where the river makes a massive turn towards the lakes and found the need to lie on a patch of ground where the sun tossed a dappled light. I watched tree creepers and sittellas, honeyeaters and robins, and was soon rocked to sleep in the swaying shadows of the massive ironbark arms.

I woke staring into the branches, the sun several degrees lower in the sky, and the feeling that someone had been whispering while I slept. Was it the gentle river breeze, the fantail's wing, the fluttering prayer flags of the leaves, or was it all of them? The land. I felt the spine of her pressing against mine, and a mighty reassurance swept over me as it has done so many times before. You are home, you are welcome.

If we do the right thing by the land, justice and peace will flow to its people.

Don't get one of your staff to send me a letter outlining your brilliant record on Indigenous Affairs, John, you've sent me plenty of those, and don't think I'm not grateful, but I was hoping we might have a yarn together about what really makes Australia's ticker tick.

Anyway, John, I know you're planning to slip away to the Lord's Test because I've noticed a softening of the detention policy, tax cuts and help for farmers … and it's not even an election year. You're tidying the desk, aren't you, John, getting ready for the royal biographer? I notice you've done nothing for blacks, John, and don't think we aren't grateful. Kindness from people like you has always meant trouble in our camp.

THE BRIDGE NEAR
NOWA NOWA

This is what happened. You'll hear otherwise, but I was there, and so was Lofty Koczak. He's not bright but he's got eyes. You know Lofty, Victor's brother, works at the Cabbage Tree Mill.

Well, Tiny Austin says you've got to have both feet on the ground. Since when, goes Brett Armstrong. Since always, says Tiny. Bullshit, says Armo. Bullshit nothin', says Tiny. I was usin' the bridge, goes Armo. 'Zackly, says Tiny, goes fa when ya usin' the bridge. Bullshit, says Armo. Suit yaself, says Tiny, lifting his glass and turning his back, sort of deliberate and taunting.

You could see Armo just wanted to belt Tiny on the back of the head, at least smash the glass out of his hand, but even he had enough brains not to try. Tiny had four cousins in the bar, and all Armo had was his mum and uncle, his sister and a city brother, and his mate ordering counteries in the saloon.

Armo was smokin' he was that wild, swallowin' down his pride in great hard lumps. Tiny was smug, it was awful to see, but for once he had the power, and in this room, at least on this one night, at his table, he had the upper hand and couldn't help the swagger, the jaunty walk, didn't want to help it. Monday it'd be back to the mill takin' orders from the boss, Armo's old man, while Armo drove around in a damn near new Bravo twin cab 4×4 doin' just about bugger all.

So Tiny swaggered and Armo smoked.

One of Armo's mill mates, Eric, yelled at Tiny, slammed his cue down and said the whole bar was fucked. Tiny's sister, Evelyn, said Eric was fucked. Eric said she was fucked ... by everybody. That was a mistake and Eric knew it.

You could see him try to reel back the last two words, but it was too late. He'd only been tryin' to stick up for the boss's son, but it was a mistake, and when Evelyn's cousin, Reggie Wallace, smacked him a good one in the mouth, he bellowed and smashed his glass against the bar and threatened Reggie with it, but you could see his heart wasn't in it. One swipe with that glass and he'd be barred for a year and there wasn't another pub for fifty miles. Even so, it'd be touch and go. The new publican was a smooth dago from the city and might not understand the rules yet. Eric had to make a noise and smash a few things for pride's sake. Everybody expected it. But eventually he slunk out, muttering curses as he went. You mob of arseholes, I'll get you mongrels. Yeah, yeah, soft cock, goes Evelyn, which was a terrible thing to say to a man, but Eric told me later that he could feel two stray teeth with his tongue and didn't want to swallow them by accident by yelling out fuckin' mole, which involved the tongue a fair bit and could cost you for a plate and a couple of front dentures. Nearest dentist one hundred miles. Every second Tuesday. If you're not too pissed you think of those things. Cut your losses.

And Armo just muttered and glared and stalked all sulky into the saloon to join his family. He jammed his huge frame into a chair and smoked. The barmen poked their heads into the pool bar nervously, assessing the atmosphere; the publican made a show of bonhomie and business as usual in the saloon, trying to smile a weak smile of support for Armo without jeopardising his bread-and-butter trade in the pool bar. It was all politics.

Armo's mum sat rigid in her chair. She'd die for her son, die just to save his humiliation, but she was powerless too. One wrong move, one wrong word, and you could have a strike on your hands or an accidental bridge spike would go through the breaking-down saw. Stop the mill for hours. She knew that, she'd been born here. If Armo's father'd been there the power ratio might have been their way, but he wasn't and damn near everyone knew he was in Lakes shaggin' that mole from the Central, so Armo and his mum were restricted on that score, knew they couldn't even refer to him without someone bringing it up. *Where is he then? Slippin' the wick?* So, mother and son chewed chips of enamel off their teeth, comin' down so hard on the bit. Mrs Armstrong's brother-in-law was there but he was from the city and knew fuck all, you could see he thought he'd landed on another planet, and the locals saw the hairpiece – well, it was like a red darn in a brown sock, toupee, couldn't command respect in a kindergarten.

Violet, the barmaid, Mrs Armstrong's niece, dashed out to the kitchen and brought them back a big plate of calamari rings, lacka bands in batter, and Armo clamped on to one like it was Tiny's ear and tore it to bits. I always stand where I can see into the saloon, that way you can see any stray sheila what walks into the pub by mistake. Happens a bit, bein' on the highway an' that. You can see the startled look of 'em straight away, like they'd walked into a jackal's cage or somethin'. So, I saw Armo's family try all sorts of ways to eat the calamari and sip the drinks with a show of calm.

Armo's uncle did his best, tells some damn fool story about the
city, I couldn't hear it, but you could see it comin' off his lips, all
jokey and mistimed. At least he was havin' a go. Armo's sister, Tina,
was just embarrassed, she just wanted to be out of there, somewhere, anywhere, some place in Dandenong where no one knew
ya, where you could wear sunnies at night with no one laughin' at
ya. I know that Tina. Bitch.

Tiny was in the bar still shoutin' about what a great pool player
he was, doin' high fives and all that American shit and you could see
Armo was gettin' the message loud and clear. It was all over really,
apart from a bit of dust and heat and bile, hot rushes of adrenaline
still squirtin' around. Few drinks, few smokes, shoutin' the bar, all
that crap, but it was sort of back to a normal Friday night. Well,
a blue is normal too, can't remember a Friday night without one,
but people were startin' to get into the ordinary groove, slappin'
their coins on the side of the table, chalkin' cues, catchin' their
reflections in the mirrors, seein' how the gel was holdin' out, gig-
glin', swishin' the hips, that's the sheilas a'course, but I never miss
that, stirs ya, 'specially Friday night, bit of music, bit of a laugh,
few beers, women swingin' their cheeky arses ...

Anyway, I glance into the saloon and see Armo's city brother's
mate, Carl I found out later, he pushes his chair back and Armo's
mum glares at him, a what's-up-with-this-prick look, but he just
barges past and out the saloon door. I see Armo's mum's lips move
like cracks in a shingle: Who is that cunt? Plain as day you can
see it. Armo's city brother tries to explain but she looks away. The
solidarity is broken, the determined retention of pride, you know
their way of saving face. Look, Armo's old man didn't own the mill,
he was just the foreman, but in a town like this it was the most

respected position apart from the publican: you couldn't cross either of them without risking your whole way of life.

But Armo's brother's city mate broke the truce. Left the table. Next minute he barges into the pool bar, and I couldn't see him proper because as he throws the door open he knocks Evelyn arse-over while she's carrying a countery and two pots. There's chips and beer everywhere. Evelyn hits the deck and you could see her mouth open to begin a decent bloody assault, when we both spy the barrel at the same time.

Armo's brother's city mate, this Carl prick, has been out to the ute and got his gun. He pushes open the door and shoots Tiny fair and square in the guts and then walks out, and we all hear the ute start up and screech off towards Lakes. Tiny is cactus. Who brought that Carl cunt into it? What's his fuckin' trouble?

The blackfellas all go wild, you know, their cuz is as good as dead, an' there's wails an' screams an' threats, well, not too many threats, what's the use? Reggie pulls out his car keys and stands in the doorway and you can see him thinkin', what's the use? The publican's on the phone, and he's white as shithouse pasta an' he's thinkin' this will cost him a few days trade ... until the funeral, when it'll pick up again.

I glance over and Armo's mum is still at the table and she's glarin' at Armo's city brother, not sayin' a bloody word. Armo is lookin' at his beer, thinkin' Oh shit, knowin' that when his old man hitched up his pants and got back to town there'd be hell to pay. No work for at least three days, coppers sneakin' around, super payout, all sorts of shit.

Barry Baker turns up and gets the doors locked, scares the publican shitless, and takes us out the front of the pub one at a time.

Takes me first, the prick. Typical copper. We stand there and he lights two fags and gives one to me. Who'd he see do that, Pierce Brosnan or someone? He was always full of shit.

Alright, Possum, he goes, what's the story? I smoke his cigarette: why not? I'm lookin' at Armo's ute parked right in front of us, the tray backed up to the verandah. You can read his shitty stickers. *Mountain Cattlemen. Save the Bush, Kill a Greenie. No Fear. Valvoline. I'm a Shooter and I Vote. Keep This Our Flag Forever. If This Ute is Rockin', Don't Laugh, It Could Be Your Daughter Inside.*

How can they bear to put all that shit on a perfectly good ute?

Well, goes Baker, what's the story?

I was tryin' to work it out into a sentence that wouldn't dob in no one, even Armo, though I hated his skin like the rest of us, but Reggie Wallace came out of the pool bar door. I told you to fuckin' stay inside, goes Baker, tryin' for all the world to sound like Rod Steiger in *Midnight Cowboy*. But Reggie just stands there. Barry, goes Reggie, you better shut up and listen, that ute hit a tree near the Toorloo Arm bridge, dead as a maggot. Lake cops on the phone now, wanna talk to you.

While he's in there, the ambulance turns up, the schoolteacher from Tostaree and some other poofter, in all their flash clobber, and I can see them in there tryin' to do somethin' for me cousin, but what's the use, his guts is out, he hit the floor dead, we all knew that. Reggie is still in the doorway watchin' the ambos and I can see him sort of slumpin', slidin' down the door, and so I take his arm. Alright cuz, I say, can't think of nothin' else, but I can see Mrs Armstrong had her head in her hands. The city brother is screamin' out, How'd I know he was a fruit loop, don't blame me, he had a ute, how else was I goin' ta get down for Tina's twenty-first? Don't blame me! Armo was just starin' at him.

Evelyn was tearing lumps out of her hair and I hooked an arm around her as she spun past. Take it easy, sista, I said. Fucked if I knew what to say to any of 'em. I've got Evelyn under one arm, her bitin' me shoulder, hard, true, teeth like a barracouta, and Reggie's sort of slumped in me other arm, an' Baker gets off the phone and turns to stare at me. First murder we've had here for years. Wrong time. This'll make the papers like when young Jaden got killed in Moe. We'll all be in shit. Five hundred thousand reconciliationists cross the Sydney Harbour Bridge on Sunday and the first blackfella to be shot is in Nowa Nowa. Tiny Austin was gunna be famous and so was Evelyn – she wouldn't be able to resist all them microphones and cameras – Mrs Armstrong knew she was going to be famous too, and the mill; the publican knew the pub was going to be famous but wasn't sure if he'd lose the licence or get rich selling grog to the curious. The journos'd give up on Lofty after the first few grunts, and I could see Baker thinkin' Carl had just shot the bolt on his promotion to Deer Park. No one, 'part from us, gave a fuckin' thought for Tiny, or his three nippers, or his mum, my aunty, who had seen too many blackfellas die like this, she was sick of it, sick to death of the violence, the beer-breath bullshit.

Baker was still lookin' at me as if he expected me to do somethin' about it all. I don't want no more trouble, Possum, it wasn't Armo's fault, right, Tiny's neither, just that prick from the city, an' he's dead, so can you just get it all settled down for a bit?

Me?

'Course you, who else can keep a lid on this mob?

It's me cousin.

I fuckin' know that, Possum, I fuckin' know who's who. Just get your mob to treat it as the fuckin' accident it is.

It's not an accident, Barry, an' you know it ... it's part of the war.

He just stared at me. Opened and shut his mouth a couple of times as he went to speak and thought better of it and then said, War bullshit.

I dunno what made me mention the war, it just came to me an' I said it. I'd been readin' all the papers, listenin' to all the news, an' well, that's how it seems to me, a last stray bullet in the last days of the war. A frightened man's bullet by a crazy soldier who wasn't sure if his side had won.

No one's won. No one ever does. It'll take years to forget. Aunt will have to die, Evelyn, Mrs Armstrong, Armo, Tina, Reggie, me, we'll all have to die, an' then our kids and then that's when things'd start gettin' back to normal, an' even then people will catch each other's eye on opposite sides of the Nowa Nowa pub on a Friday night. Take more than a stroll on the bridge to fix that.

AN ENEMY OF
THE PEOPLE

Many people think I'm a traitor. You're not like the rest of them, they tell me, you're not *really* Aboriginal.

What they say has cool logic. Clinical analysis of genes says I'm more Cornish than Koorie. I hardly ever suffered racist remarks, and experienced no disadvantage, due to my heritage.

My sister and I would never have gone to university if it hadn't been for the then prime minister, because our parents could never have afforded it, and yet we both got that chance and the economic security and esteem it provided. So, no, I'm not like a real Aborigine, because if I'd been blacker my opportunities would probably have been curtailed. There would have been even less money in the house, the expectations of my teachers and parents may have been fewer, my job opportunities crippled. The only impediment I faced was economic. My only real struggle was with the knowledge that a whole side of our history had been deliberately painted out.

People can't understand why you would identify with a culture so seemingly remote. It's a common theme in pubs and kitchens when pale Koories are discussed. Why do they do it? Are they on a lurk? These suspicions become rumours fuelled by ultra-right nationalists and discreetly fanned by the government. But we are not just the product of our parents' house, there's the influence of grandparents and great-grandparents and a whole history of jumbled heritage. Australians were never a pure race, as Geoffrey Blainey and co. like to think. The mix happened first on the frontier and at every national intersection since. The Anglos were mixed with the Celts, and both were changed by Indigenous genes and the country on which they ate their bread, the ground where the grain for that bread was grown.

Since then, the mix has continued. Purity is not in race but in purpose. I just want to respect all the roads where my ancestors set foot. What made my grandmother, mother and father the extraordinary people they were?

Australians find it upsetting, a kind of betrayal, when light-skinned people identify with their indigeneity. I can think of dozens of prominent Aboriginal and Torres Strait Islander politicians, activists, artists, writers, musicians, nurses, teachers and train drivers who have all suffered the charge of not being a *real* Aborigine. Why should they be denied what the Irish, Greek and Jewish diaspora celebrate at the drop of a baklava, Guinness or gefilte fish? Especially if you are in your own country and in touch every day with the land that breathes its soul into your nostrils each time you wake.

It disappoints a lot of my friends and associates that I want to correct what I see as their ignorance of Australian history past and present. I've been abused by hoteliers, bosses, cricket crowds, and lost some friends because of it.

Speaking of cricket crowds, I must pay homage to the president of the Lorne Football and Cricket Club. In 1997 he chastised his own supporters, who'd thought it amusing to yell out the n-word every time I faced a ball. He strode to the middle of the Lorne cricket oval, trembling with rage, and said, 'Mate, can I go and punch those blokes in the head?'

'No,' I replied. 'Thanks for the offer, but I'd prefer to bat all day.'

Now, I bat like Eddie the Eagle skis, but it's amazing what you can do when inspired.

And anyway, mate, I didn't see you after the game, but thanks, I've never forgotten it. I like to think of you as the best Australians can become. Fair. Truly accepting people for themselves, not what school they went to or the colour of their grandmother's skin.

But I'm afraid not everyone is as generous as the man from Lorne. I've made many friends through sport, half of them from the opposing sides. I've met the ironic wink from an opposition player in three foot of mud at Birregurra, as if to say *this kind of behaviour is certifiable, don't you reckon?*

I've sat yarning well after the sun has set over Hayley's Reef at Apollo Bay discussing the finer points of fishing and cricket with blokes I'd hate to lose as friends. I'd hate for those men to think of me as a nark or a man who hated his country and country-men. I don't, quite the opposite; love of my country and its people hurts, it is so strong. I just can't stand by and watch decent peo-ple fail to understand how great their country is and how great we as a people might become. Doug Lang, Warren Riches, Dennis Dare, John Gorwell, Steve Morsehead, Brian Noseda, Waldo Garner, Dave Nelson, Blondie Parker, Barry Parker, Pussy Rippon, Sparra Harrison, Merv Brady, Guy Permezel, Tommy Lloyd, John Armstrong, Gerry Menke, Curl Shaw, it'd crush me if you thought I was a nark. After all this time, all those good yarns. It'd hurt very deeply not to be able to front up with the same ease and enjoy a few beers and bit of bullshit. There are a few other names I'd like to put there too, but my brothers, you are Aboriginal. Some of you know it and deny it, some don't care and some simply don't know because your mother made me promise not to tell. See the gulf denial of our past has opened between us?

If we did this properly, it could become the national celebration of our greatness rather than the slinking, suspicious pig-headed repudiation of 120,000 years of connection to this land. So many of us have a link to the world's oldest culture and deny it. Most of the rest are within a bee's eyebrow of admitting the crushing weight of love pressing on their chests: the massive love for the land. The only impediment to accepting the full embrace of the country's love is our inability to look over our shoulder, our failure to shape up to our lingering dread of exposure. If we can learn history we can embrace the past, and for many it will be an embrace of family denied.

Most Australians, however, view those who discover their Indigenous ancestry late in life like those who recover lost memories: people to be treated with circumspection, if not scorn. Both recoveries have been used by impostors, but are Australians just looking for an excuse to dismiss the discomforting fact in the same way we've excused our treatment of refugees? If some of them are not genuine, then we can dismiss the lot as charlatans! Too easy, my countrymen and women, unworthy of your finer inclinations.

I would like to think that in Australia we could rest an elbow on the bar or sit at the table and crook our fingers through the handle of our teacups and discuss these matters, but it is impossible because of the incredulity with which most Australians greet the knowledge of our shared history.

During the 2005 Eureka celebrations I listened to most of ABC Radio National's comprehensive coverage at Ballarat and the broadcast of historical lectures: the role of women, the English–Irish conflict, the Irish–Irish conflict, rich versus poor, the democratic fervour, it was all fascinating. Aborigines? Nothing. Invisible. Nothing to do with democracy, identity or history.

Years ago I worked as director of the Australian Studies Project of the Commonwealth Schools Commission and was awed by the bilingual publishing program at Yuendumu. They produced these stunning educational tools on an old Fordigraph machine. I went back to Canberra and prepared a shortlist of the educational programs in Australia most deserving of Commonwealth assistance. Yuendumu was at the top of the list. I sat dumbfounded during the meeting while the public servants re-shuffled the list to bring in an application by an elite Queensland school that wanted funding to add two rowing shells to the eight they possessed. Yuendumu did not get funded, and I wrote my letter of resignation as the meeting continued.

It's too easy to attack the conservatives in the United States or Australia for the current state of world behaviour. People bear responsibility for the moral tone of their country, and when the best-educated people in the land are blinded by ignorance of their country's history, how can we blame politicians when they pander to our selfishness? It wouldn't have mattered greatly if the Liberals or Humphrey Bear had won the last three federal elections.

We are fortunate to live in a democracy where it is within our power to tell our elected representatives what we want. Why do we limit the application of pressure on Canberra to changing parliamentarians' superannuation allowances or sacking ministers who take their lovers on overseas trips at public expense? What about a couple of polite questions when 353 desperate people drown within sight of our surveillance aircraft? Why not ask, politely, why we can give one billion to the 2004 tsunami, and deserving of every cent, yet allow trachoma and kidney failure to remain at higher levels in Indigenous Australia than in Bangladesh?

We have to ask those questions; it is our responsibility. Liberal, Labor? Hardly matters. I remember when Graham Richardson, the Minister for Aboriginal Affairs in the Keating government, got his photo on the front page of every daily newspaper in the country two weeks out from an election. He had his arm around the shoulders of a senior Utopia woman after promising that a Labor government would deliver running water to her community. Labor won that election, but Utopia still did not get the promised water supply. What happened, Graham? Lose the memo? Or did you just do whatever it takes to win and then move on? Footage of Senator balance-of-power Brian Harradine trying to dance with Yolngu people was just as sickening. Don't dance, senator, because having expressed what you think of Aboriginal people you should have been denied that opportunity. No, Senator Richard Alston, Aboriginal people didn't invent the wheel; nor did they invent the rack, the gas chamber or tax evasion.

It's what we believe that counts. I'm an agnostic, but I'd quite happily settle for a country that operated exclusively according to the Ten Commandments. You couldn't go wrong truly believing that all of us were created in God's image and loving our neighbours as ourselves. You couldn't go wrong with belief that strong. So how is it, politicians, that you can express such passion for the word of the Lord and enact the legislation you do?

But it doesn't matter what Canberra thinks. It's us, the people, who really count – those with a chance to share a pot of beer or a cup of tea with others, the chance to seek out knowledge and promote it and to indulge the better side of our natures, the side that fervently believes in equality, that Australia's fundamental commitment is that everyone deserves a fair go. Where is our thirst for uncompromised knowledge? Why do we encourage politicians to lie to us?

Australians aren't the problem. We prove time and again that we have good hearts, that we can reach out a hand to the needy. Our problem stems from our national myopia, and that arises from the history intelligent people still insist on teaching impressionable children.

We must investigate our past with rigour, but not abuse people for the views they hold; instead we must strive to make our national education as comprehensive as possible. I've been to meetings of the Australian Literary Translators' Association (ALITRA), the organisation that dispenses money for the translation of languages other than English, and been greeted with good-mannered bemusement when I requested that it spend some of its funds on Aboriginal translations. The members thought I was joking. There was only one Aboriginal language, no one spoke it, and in any case there wasn't a literature!

I was trying to argue the case to have some of the Walpiri and Arrente stories translated into English so they could be taught in the community schools and to all Australians. The bemusement was genuine. I had it explained to me that I must have misunderstood because the funds are for *migrant* languages – Greek, Hebrew, Chinese, Vietnamese, Italian, French. The ALITRA charter does not make that distinction, but people were incredulous that I had misunderstood the *intent* of the charter. I knew exactly what the intent was, and it arose from the blindness that has our country stumbling in a fog of displacement and denial.

In 2002 I was at the national linguists' conference. Aboriginal participants were involved in sideshows to the conference while the linguists described the brilliance of their research. I wandered into a session by mistake. I was lost. I realised my mistake after a while and prepared to leave – until I realised the linguists were discussing the copyright of their material and the methods for including research as properties in a will. Bequeathing Aboriginal languages to their children!

Not all linguists work like that, but there were plenty of greedy ears in this seminar, and the attitude has resulted in major court cases, including disputation over the ownership of Strehlow's vault of artefacts and recordings. The linguists were surprised to hear that some found this discussion immoral. Researchers need to protect their work from predatory publishers or unethical rivals, but it is a dangerous precedent to divide other people's cultural heritage as if it is a brick veneer in Balwyn.

In 2004 I found myself in discussion with the inheritor of a document of 700 pages of Wathaurong language. The woman who compiled it had said she would give it to the community after her death. The son wanted copyright. He wanted to sell the language back to the people from whom it was twice taken. Ronald Biggs would have been impressed.

Not all news is as bleak or dangerous to the national soul. In an important breakthrough in 2005, Aretha Briggs, Doris Paton, Lyn Dent and Heather Bowe sat down together and drew up a plan for the Victorian Curriculum Assessment Authority to introduce Indigenous Victorian languages into the Year 12 VCE curriculum, a massive effort. Aretha, Doris and Lyn are descended from a long line of wise warrior men and women; I don't know much about Heather's background, except that she's a decent Australian with plenty of courage and no guilt. So, four good Australians get together to share their vision to advance Australian education by a light year. Why does it seem so confusing and treacherous for the rest of us?

The confusion about what defines a language other than English goes right to the heart of our national identity, right to the heart of the muddled way we represent ourselves here and overseas, why we sit in awe while New Zealand rugby players, white and black, perform a haka. Do you want something to perform at the MCG, the SCG, the Gabba and the WACA? Well, it'd be slightly different in every state because it would depend on *where* the ground was, whose land it was on, but if we looked we'd find a warrior song for that soil. It wouldn't have the same ferocious bellicosity of the Maori (that's something else our country could learn), but it would say everything there was to know about the power of place and the great heroes who fought for it. It would even celebrate the famed Merri Creek mud from which the centre square of the MCG is constructed. Imagine the richness and flavour that would add to the traditional chicken lunch at the Boxing Day Test. I'm not being ironic, I'm seriously patriotic.

I can see it now on Grand Final Day: two footy teams and a few token white representatives lining up to sing the national anthem and perform a Woiwurrung warrior song. No nation anywhere else on the face of the earth could do it; people would switch on

TV sets in Berlin, Paris, London, Toronto and Los Angeles just to see this unique expression of national identity.

We live in a seriously compromised country, but why have we let it become such a problem? We should relish the complexity, the depth, the length of the history; we should feel a tiny bit smug that we know things people from other countries don't, things they find strange, exotic and compelling. Let's bury the stone and steel hatchets and fall in love with our country. Let's share the guiltless embrace of true love. It will require selflessness and reckless courage, unstinting respect for each other, time and endurance. But it's worth it. Nations are built this way.

TRACKS

HONEYPOT TWO SHOTS TWO POTS AND MISS HERMANSBERG

I knew I was in a story the moment the gum leaf came out, and I began to worry how to tell it.

And I was doubly convinced as soon as I saw Miss Hermansberg lean close to the Old Man and whisper in his ear. Not because she's lewd, not because the Old Man was inviting intimacy, but because it's how women at Hermansberg speak. Their voices can be drowned when a dove shuffles its wings.

She might have fit the name Miss Hermansberg once. A fair sort of time ago. Before the belly and the grey roots. But the dimples in the centre of her cheeks would have been causing blokes sleepless nights, and the eyes, well, the eyes still work, and of course the grace. She walks as if she's balancing an egg white on a beer coaster on her head.

She leans towards the Old Man and breathes an intoxicating story in his ear. The strangest, sorriest story a country can conjure, but I can't begin it because the Old Man is the strangest, most complicated bunch of bones you would ever meet in a lifetime of London buses. Not that he's been to London, but I'm trying to indicate his rareness, the impossibility of his talents and peculiarities.

It's not everyone who plays an alarming repertoire of songs on a gum leaf. He's very good and made even more incredible by his ability – well, not ability, but predilection I suppose – to play it at the oddest times. Like today, at an art gallery in Port Hedland. Putting 'art gallery' and 'Port Hedland' within a single word of each other might seem to be testing the faith between reader and writer, but there is a gallery there, and the Old Man stood smack in the centre of the floor, bringing to a complete stop any chance the staff had to finish the installation of an exhibition of Kariyarra art and bringing to a premature close the piano rehearsal of Chopin by a teenage girl of Indian-Malay extraction. She was good, too, and beautiful, and her father waiting to take her home was handsome and urbane, but he had to wait and she had to sit with her hands spread across five octaves because, as a way of exciting the gallery to the possibilities of art, the Old Man had leapt into gum-leaf renditions of 'Blue Bayou', 'Moonlight Becomes You', 'Numeralla Pines', 'The Old Rugged Cross' and 'Streets of Old Fitzroy'. I told you it was alarming.

But everybody stopped just where they were because with a bloody leaf pinched off a dusty, half-starved gum at the front door he hit every note as if with a diamond hammer, swept into a few glissades and tremolos, and inserted the blues into songs that had never expected to hear themselves as anything but sugared cream.

The art gallery is a converted shed with a shitty old particle board ceiling, but the sound was fat and round and smooth. People were transfixed: holding lighting battens, clutching a large bouquet of flowers meant for a vase at the end of the hall, but on the wrong side of the Old Man so that the shortish woman kept shifting them from one side of her chest to the other so the gladioli didn't remove her nasal polyps. The rather grand dame, caught mid-gesture in the centre of the room, directly in line for every blast of air from the leaf, will probably be grander when she's dressed for the grand opening. She spells it 'grande'. The artists are Aboriginal and there's no way some of them aren't going to turn up in check flannelette shirts and thongs; their best check shirt and thongs given a douse in the sink, but flannelette and thongs nonetheless.

But it's Port Hedland and the grand dame is possibly the bank manager's wife, or maybe the retired head of the girls' school. I can't tell, but how could I? What I can tell is that she is going to get dolled up because there are two or three chances in Port Hedland and one of them is the Camel Cup and no one else would include it as a chance. Well, not quite true, four other women do, but the rest go for the lightweight frock and the slip-on flatties.

How do I know that if I can't tell whose wife she is? Well, put it down to experience in enough country towns to make me certain.

But look, she was halfway through a stagey sweep of the arm to embrace all the art treasures of Port Hedland when the Old Man stole her oxygen so he could force it across the membrane of a reluctant eucalypt. Everybody had stopped mid-stride, mid-gesture, mid-installation. All except me, because I saw it coming and made myself comfortable on a milk crate in front of *Untitled II (gouache and red sand)*.

The Old Man had time afterwards for a fairly comprehensive summary of Victorian Aboriginal history, and the spell would have remained unbroken except a bird of paradise attempted eye surgery on the shortish woman whose arms were obviously not up to a recital of timeless gum-leaf melodies and a history of a state she wouldn't recognise in an atlas but for the habit of atlas makers to print the name of states in bold serif type. VICTORIA.

The shortish woman discarded the brief attempt to fish Victoria's shape and position from her mind because the lurid shaft of the flower caused her to sneeze. The spray of Cecil Brunner rose-buds flopped to the floor and was speckled like a hen's egg in red dust. Well, it was Port Hedland.

But that was earlier. What's happening now is that Miss Hermansberg is outlining the history of her own state, which has the shape of a rather stiff and tufted muffin. Miss Hermansberg knows she hasn't got long because the Old Man is opening and shutting his mouth in an attempt to elaborate on the old days by the Snowy, so she prunes her history, keeping it spare and bald, but a history such as this must take some time. A story of a woman shot in the back by police officers of the realm within gaze of her children, the older girl holding the baby and the boy the billy because it was what he'd been told to grab whenever trouble threatened. Which it did frequently because this was Australia and Australians could find all sorts of reasons why a woman has to be shot in the back in front of her children. Of course, we don't do that now.

Miss Hermansberg was the baby, and when pressed probably can't be sure whether she remembers all the details of that day or has been schooled in them by her older sister, who at the time was pregnant to the stationowner's son even though she was only eleven. But there was a good reason for that, too. Probably because eleven-year-old girls are so promiscuously seductive. Something to do with the packs of swap cards, broken biscuits and tennis balls they carry in the pockets of their school shorts. It pays to carry your own tennis ball because the school can never be guaranteed to have enough money to supply equipment for spontaneous games of handball or brandy. Because this is Australia.

She gets very close to the end of the story and the Old Man reaches for the leaf in his top pocket, but Honeypot claps her hands in delight at the presentation of another pot of Emu Bitter.

'Come on, come on,' shouts Honeypot, 'bring it on.' She has a striking voice, but the most striking thing about the voice is that for three days she's been sitting next to Miss Hermansberg and Sunflower and saying nothing and casting her gaze down from an expressionless face. Sunflower – yes, I know I didn't mention Sunflower, but you try and fit it into the title.

Sunflower is beautiful. Christ, everyone's beautiful in this story. Sunny is a big girl but her face is still rather gorgeous, and lit by a daunting intelligence. Doesn't matter how big you get, a handsome face crowned by a coronet of curled hair in a pleasant shade of ginger is still worth a look. But crikey, she is a big girl. The night before, at the impromptu women's pool tournament, she wrenched her knee and had to sit through today's meeting with an ice pack pressed to it, rather like a big ham on shaved ice in a butcher's window.

But Sunflower has been single-handledly – if you don't count Miss Hermansberg and Honeypot – resisting the new tide of racism released by the government on any unsuspecting black individual forced into the court system of our most northern state, the Flying Muffin.

Sunny is saying nothing because she's twisting the top off a 150ml bottle of Hardy's Special Reserve. Drinking makes her serious. More serious. She doesn't even look up when Honeypot screams, 'Bring it on, Uncle Jacky Jacky!'

Miss Hermansberg and Honeypot had taken to calling the Old Man Uncle Jacky Jacky because unlike every other conference attendee he refused to wear a nametag. Surely everybody knew his name! Well, everybody but Miss Hermansberg and Honeypot, because they'd only met him once and clutched at the thing that struck them most. He gave them a recital of Jacky Jacky at the baggage carousel in Port Hedland. Well, 'carousel' is bullshit because it's just an old steel trailer with two odd tyres.

Anyway, we men had been in the pub for hours, conducting a refreshing survey of important issues, when the triumvirate of court assistants turned up and spied the Old Man sitting beneath an advertisement for Jack Daniel's bourbon: 'Jack sat here.' They think it's funny, and I suppose it is in its own way, but we blink up at them like owls because we think we've just sorted a structure for the enculturation, or re-enculturation, of every willing boy in Victoria. Wouldn't you blink like an owl?

But Honeypot is on a mission. 'Four hours I've got. Bring it on. Get me the grog, Uncle Jacky Jacky. Four hours and I'm back in the bush.'

And the bush she means is the alcohol-free community where the government allows residents to buy fuel if they can prove they have washed their faces twice a day. Australia's a tidy town.

She's almost capering with excitement, and I can't take my eyes off the sight because this is the shy girl who you could have been forgiven for thinking was a mute.

And she's black, as black as you ever see people. There's a lustre, a dark lustre, that reminds me of the back of a mussel shell that has been scoured to such a degree that the nacre begins to gleam in a sheen of opalescence. You look for the colours but can't quite pick them because they're not quite there. The skin is black, so black it shines, and you think you see a little shimmer of ebony pearl. Christ, she's beautiful.

She's wearing an old windcheater with arms so long the cuffs roll over her hands and she has to keep flicking them back. The grace of this movement is astonishing. When she picks up the pool cue and addresses the white ball, men's jaws drop. Well, they are miners from the Western Desert, even though they're philosophically opposed to black people. Well, it is Australia. But Christ, she's beautiful.

She spins on her feet and casts her gaze quickly this way and that, looking for the next opportunity to embrace the world.

I don't mind, I'm an old man. I can gaze at beauty when I please. I'm in awe of the transformation from shy desert girl to bold young woman on the tear. But as she sweeps and jives from pool game to our table, flicking her elegant wrists and scooping up brand-new drinks with whoops of delight, we hear her story from Sunflower, with judicious interpolated whispers from Miss Hermansberg, and are in no doubt that if anyone in the Lucky Country has a right to have one night a year on the tear it is our very own Honeypot, who becomes Honeypot Two Shots because of her increasing ability to give away two shots. She's a deadly pool player despite having to flick her cuffs away from her wrists every other second. No one can jive around the table and whoop and scream with laughter and keep the white ball under control all the time.

The Old Man launches into Jacky Jacky, deftly calculated to send Honeypot Two Shots into laughter mid-shot. In, off. Two shots. Miss Hermansberg is hiding behind her hands, her shoulders trembling with laughter. Her eyes peek above her fingers and she giggles like a girl, fifty years after she was a girl, but I'll be surprised if that remarkable lustre ever leaves those eyes until they are shaded by shovels of red sand. Miss Hermansberg's eyes glint with discreet and modest mischief.

The mining lad, gauche in denim work shorts and dusty socks rolled above his boots, becomes desperate with her gleeful allure and makes a clumsy and inelegant suggestion, an ejaculation of desperation and hope, but what can you expect, he's just out of the desert. The Australian subterranean desert mole gets one chance a year to mate, and Desert Boy has fewer. He sees this as his chance, but really it's a mistake.

I haven't mentioned the Goanna and the Dancer. The Goanna has smoked something that causes him to grasp the jukebox like you would the shoulders of a favourite aunt, and his body is weaving like a goanna. Lost in the sweet rhythm of Troy Cassar Daly. The Dancer, possibly the funniest man on the planet, has dropped into a reverie, which he is wont to do when thinking. What, a black man thinking in Australia? Well, yes, he is, and if you didn't know you'd think he was morose, but he's just thinking, and he's leaning back against a pillar, deliberately removing himself from our gaze. He also happens to have been the Australian under-nineteen boxing champion ten years ago, so for Desert Boy to make inappropriate remarks to Honeypot Two Shots is a mistake he doesn't know he's made. Goanna is still locked in embrace with the jukebox and the Stiff Gins but if Desert Boy had realised he was part of the Miss Hermansberg, Honeypot Two Shots, Sunflower, Uncle Jacky Jacky and Silly Old Bookman show, he would have clamped his jaw shut after seeing the Goanna's bull neck and chest like a keg of beer, even if he, Desert Boy, was in the thrall of imminent orgasm.

But he didn't know, and it didn't matter, because Honeypot Two Shots darted her hand out of her cuff into a lovely declination from the wrist, and the fingers curved as one in a gesture towards poor old Desert Boy. Of course, the loveliness of that hand broke his heart and ruptured his groin.

'You think I have to suck up to you for a drink, eh? You think, black girl crawlin' roun' for her grog. I'm not gunna crawl for a man. I got a man back 'ome, I got kids. One night I got to drink with Ol' Uncle Jacky Jacky and silly ol' Bookman, one chance to whip ol' Bookman's arse at pool, and no lil' fella like you gunna stop me, eh. You wanna play pool, get a grip of ya cue, boy, or piss off.'

Well, she was a bit pissed, but brazen defiance became her.

Desert Boy gulped and picked up his cue. The Dancer peered around the column and his arms bowed unconsciously into the shape offering the gloves for lacing. The Goanna looked back over his shoulder and gave Desert Boy a frightening look. How dare he interrupt the Mills Sisters.

The barman called last drinks in a gloomy voice, seemingly resigned to the hopelessness of his mission.

Honeypot Two Shots swept down on him and began purchasing alcohol in bulk. She dropped two cans of Coke in front of Miss Hermansberg, who had already explained to Uncle Jacky Jacky why she didn't drink, and clinked two pots together in each hand, dangling one pair before Uncle Jacky Jacky and at someone stupid enough to tell stories on paper. The other two were for her; Honeypot Two Shots Two Pots.

But soon we were bushed. Uncle Jacky Jacky retired gracefully to a bed of the softest gum leaves, Bookman went to his room and drank three glasses of the worst water in Christendom. Well, it was Port Hedland. Meanwhile, the Goanna, the Dancer, Honeypot Two Shots Two Pots, Miss Hermansberg, Car Doors and Lizard Lady took a bottle of Scotch and two bottles of Coke out to the swimming pool. I know I haven't mentioned Car Doors and Lizard Lady, and I'm not going to. I'm too tired. And besides, Lizard Lady is the second-most courageous person on the planet and deserves her own story where her tubby figure is not lost in the effulgence of Honeypot Two Shots Two Pots. But they were there, Car Doors pouring bumper Scotches and smacking his lips with great delectation, Lizard Lady just loving life.

But that's when the world went black because Bookman was snuggled down in his feather bed. Feathers, bullshit – it was Port Hedland.

Anyway, next morning Bookman finds Honeypot Two Shots Two Pots alarmingly refreshed and bending her lustrous face over the letters pages of *The Australian*. Like watching Naomi Campbell turn into a librarian. Goodness, we live in a funny country.

A LETTER TO MARLO

You know how in my last story I said I was trying to tell nothing but the truth? Well, this one is the truth too. If you believe my eyes, heart and brain. Which you'd be unwise to do. Completely.

And you know I said it's for you, well, I lied already. It's for your mum because you are only one, not even that. It is for you as well, of course, because I was thinking of you all the time; there are a lot of babies in Maningrida. But mostly this is for your mother because she's got a really good heart and a huge capacity to love. As you know. And she's Australian. As you are. And me. Which is where the problem starts.

I don't want to depress you, either of you, but you know how in the first place white people lied, cheated, murdered, raped, pillaged, judged and slandered Aboriginal people? And that was just the fervent Christians; the Scots of stingingly moral rigidity and the Irish so determined to fight for freedom, and the English who would bleed rather than break the law ... sorry, Marlo, get your mother to explain it. Well, those people were our ancestors, so you can see we came from very upright stock, but somewhere along the line our deep aversion to black people had a hiatus, which is a bit like a hernia, but during that hiatus someone took their pants down and had sexual congress with the despised. Probably twice. Not the same woman and probably a different man. Get your mother to explain it.

Anyway, you'll find you've got relations from Hobart to Lockhart River. It's a dog's breakfast. But if you're going to tell the truth and live by it, you have to watch closely, think carefully and speak only as often as your brain has completely resolved all of life's complex tapestry ... ah, forget that too, no one likes a mute, except Louis Armstrong. Get your father to explain that.

Oh, and speaking of dogs, I'm a dog wrangler for a vet. I catch 'em, he cures 'em. Which is another thing the white people hate. They want all the Yolgnu dogs killed. Despite the fact that this is Dog Dreaming country. But whites love their dogs and look after them. See the difference? The blackfella dogs have mange and fleas and ovaries. The black flea and mange are European imports into Australia, although no one paid the tax. So we're here to treat the mange and remove the ovaries of bitches and the Jatz crackers of dogs. If we can catch them.

Of course, the white people come to get their dogs treated too. For nothing. Whites are good at corruption. And their dogs have the same diseases. Fancy that. But they love their dogs more. See, Marlo?

Yes, I know, I'm sounding terse, bitter, unyielding, unfair. I'm *trying* to tell the truth, but it's complex. The problem is that someone in our family took their pants off, which we know is wicked, and then someone else in the family remembered those pants and their proximity to the ground, and then we had to say we either believe in those pants or we don't.

Well, I wasn't sure whether I believed, but some people told me this and some told me the other and just when we thought this is how it all works my cousin says no, it can't, it has to work like this. But it was too late for me, I'd got all bound up and wrapped around by the sticky webs of black story ... and Australian history, which I was shocked to discover I knew nothing about, despite having studied it at Australia's best university, some say one of the best in the world. Won't it come as a shock to all those professors to find they've been peddling crap with less credibility than scientology. Get your father to explain about scientology, it's best if I don't get started.

But Marlo, I hope you can see the problem with a conflicted, some say confused, heart. Maningrida is a long way north and I'm a mere dog wrangler with a filthy shirt, so a lot of the white people treated me as if I was a piece of poo and most of the blackfellas are just sick of *balanda* and don't treat me with much at all.

But as a dog wrangler with a dirty shirt I was able to sit back and look because no one asked me anything, no one expected anything I had to say to bear one gram of sense. Pretty bloody good guess, if you ask me. But in the watching I saw the astounding arrogance of *balanda* when speaking to the inscrutable black face of the Yolgnu. You only needed to hear the words 'bottom line' to know that some black fingers were being rapped.

The young woman in the halter top with the midriff bared was twirling her skirts about like some hot-shot media adviser, but it was a lot worse than that – she was an arts administrator and she could barely keep contempt from her voice. She winked at me conspiratorially. 'These people, what can you do with them?'

Half-arsed mechanics' boys speak to black Elders with sarcasm dripping off their tongues. Shopkeepers avoid looking at black and try to chum up with whites, perceived whites, in dirty shirts. Until you don't wink back or refuse to be served before the black woman who has been waiting for ten minutes.

Which makes me an old brindle hero, doesn't it, Marlo? No, little mate, just someone a bit shocked by what he sees. And a bit frissoned by the delicious luxury of watching, of being ignored.

The tough lady administrator is laying down the fiscal law to a grandfather whose exclusive right it is to tell five-twelfths of the Dog Dreaming. She can add up and he knows the workings of the universe. So how come he can't understand that there's been a new flash of inspiration in government and all money for bilingual education has been whisked away so that the evils of his culture can be forgotten? Got it, old man? Well, that's how it is. Today. Tomorrow, who knows? I'm just the administrator, Sambo; I'm just here to see the Australian government's will is implemented. And go to Paris for lunch.

Am I irascible, Marlo? Ask your grandmother. Don't ask if I am irascible, just ask what it means. Am I a bitter bigot? That's what I ask myself, Marlo, because I can't help watching these magnificent white administrators and their contempt for the people they are remunerated to serve.

The first white people came here in 1956, and that's just sixty-five years before you were born. The lady missionary was aghast at their nakedness, and gave them each a piece of red cloth to keep them modest, and so they wore them as head and neck scarves. The man who skippered the boat to bring the news of God to these people later became famous because he could use a beer box as a drum. Talented man. So they made him governor. You know, it makes sense.

Marlo, of course there are good white people up here. The sewerage maintenance man married a Yolgnu woman and is sensitive to the culture; the visiting vet refuses to put down a dog without the consent of its owner. All the white people are going, 'Kill the dogs, kill the dogs?' The truth is, Marlo, there's a shitload of dogs but the people *are* bringing their dogs to the vet to get spayed because they've learnt after five years to trust him and so in another five years, if the government can refrain from changing its mind, there won't be as many dogs and they'll be in better health.

Of course there are good white people. The lady in the women's centre speaks to black women as if they're her sisters, whereas a colleague, immensely qualified you know, can hardly keep her eyes or nostrils within range: 'Zey don't love zere dogs, zey are cruel, zey hurt zere little poppies.' She's French. Joan of Arc of dogs. Has four of her own. Gets me to load them all into the truck to get de-sexed. At Yolgnu expense. No greater love, Marlo, no greater love than a refined French woman.

And then there are the real Aussie whitefellas. In blue singlets and Akubras to prove it. The Australian flag tattooed on their dicks. Talk about tough. One of them runs over a Yolgnu dog and sends his missus up to tell us. The family who own the dog are stricken. Vet looks at the animal but it has massive wounds and would need plastic surgery, which we can't do. 'Waste of good money, anyway,' says the killer's girlfriend.

The family don't want to lose their dog so it is given painkillers while they make up their mind. Next morning they know the dog can't survive and I go around to pick it up. The skin has been ripped off from shoulder to toes and the abdomen is torn. It's been flayed after being dragged along by the car, which didn't stop immediately. Heroes don't. You can see how the claws attach to the foot bones. Anatomically interesting. I take the dog, the vet gives it the green dream and I dump it in a hole and shovel red dirt onto its beautiful golden coat.

Next day the killer brings his own dog in for treatment. Kennel cough. Hard to believe because whites look after their dogs so well. Guess what kind of dog Akubra man has, Marlo? Upper reaches North Manchurian mastiff. Wouldn't look out of place on a rugby field or at a mafia funeral. And he's got three of them. You know, it makes sense. They're a fashion statement. Match his nature.

There you are, Marlo, see how I did that, started finding white people to praise and ended with my keyboard awash with sarcasm. Of course that man loves his dogs. No one else has bigger or more ferocious dogs, even though they have one tiny flaw. They attack black people. Of course the French woman loves her dogs, Marlo, cuddles them, pets them, pampers them, but seems blind to the love her neighbour showers on her dogs and children.

Yesterday I went to the house next to the French woman and sedated a few dogs prior to spaying. 'No more pups,' the lady of the house declared. She was wearing a red sarong I knew she had screen-printed herself, and I can tell you, Marlo, man to baby boy, she looked a real picture.

Anyway, her daughter raced over and looked up at me and pointed to a mango tree and, there in the purple shade, all her pups were lined up in sleep, each with a tiara, earring or necklace. One had an earring attached to its navel like a body piercing. The little girl waited for my approval and I knelt and tickled their tummies and they squirmed, like only puppies can, and all the jewellery fell off and we all rolled about with laughter. Well, you had to, it was the funniest thing.

When that little girl showed me her dog art, it was such a relief to have the tension fall away. Irascible bigots tense up, Marlo, their shoulders tighten like steel hawsers straining to hold the boats of asylum-seekers to a penitentiary wharf. Ask your father to ana-lyse that last sentence, he'll notice that if irascible bigots insist on getting political at the drop of a sarcasm then they deserve tense shoulders. Anyway, puppies with bling is the cure.

Your mother would be repulsed by much that she would see here. Well, she's a nurse, and a good one. But there's rubbish everywhere up here, Marlo. Plastic bags, bent saucepans, broken toys, chip packets and soft-drink cans. No beer cans, not one. Dry community, Marlo. Imagine how I suffered. But the rubbish is unbelievable. I don't understand it, Marlo. I can't bear to pass a cigarette butt or bread tag in my own town, and here the crap is everywhere. It's raked up into piles every so often and burnt, but can you imagine what that smells like? If I go to a campsite and someone's burnt plastic in the firepit I go apoplectic. (Apoplectic, not epileptic. Your great-grandmother was epileptic. I'd never go epileptic over a bit of burnt rubbish.)

I don't understand rubbish, Marlo, but then I don't understand how a cardboard-box magnate who cheats 25 million people can be given $35 million as a reward. I don't understand it, Marlo, but I know which is morally repugnant.

I can understand all the cast-off clothes at the beach, snagged in the mangroves, rolled in coils on the tideline. This mob here believe you should cleanse the spirit of the dead by washing their possessions in the sea and never touch them again. So the shirt, the pants, the mattress all get a good salty washing. I understand that, Marlo, but is it a good look?

Now, little mate, I can feel myself getting close to the guts of it. Today at Ankabadbirra we came to an outstation beside a river and a magpie goose swamp. Do you know that the Yolgnu word for magpie goose is exactly the same as the Wathaurong word, in Victoria? Exactly. Of course, there's no magpie geese left in Victoria because the first thing the 'settlers' did was to drain the swamps and shoot any birds stupid enough to stay around. Bitterness, Marlo, bitterness; you can see that I keep sliding back into its seductive embrace. And 'foot' is the same as in Wathaurong, too. Almost all over Australia the word for foot is something like *jinnang*. That's interesting, don't you think?

Anyway, we turn up at this outstation and all the dogs howl. It's remote out here and the dogs are the intercontinental missile defence shield. '*Balanda, balanda*,' all the forty dogs bark. Three families, but forty dogs. It's still only a dog each, I suppose.

An old man emerges from beneath a frangipani and motions for us to set up under a mango tree's shade. Polite, calm, but not delirious to see *balanda* in his camp. Even if it's to treat sick or explosively fertile dogs.

There're plastic drink bottles and crap everywhere but most is raked in heaps awaiting the carcinogenic fire. Yet what you notice, as soon as you switch off the Toyota's diesel, is the silence. Well, it's not really silence because there's always a dog muttering over a bone or a computer memory stick: 'I'll eat your memory, I'll eat your memory.' Funny things, dogs.

But there's an incredible, overpowering peace here. My first instinct is to sit down and close my eyes, but that would have been a mistake because then two breathtakingly beautiful women walk out of a house and smile. I reel back at the scorch of absolute beauty – and I'm saying this, Marlo, because you're a man and it's my job to teach you about such things. All the women in Maningrida move with a grace that soothes your soul.

And these women walk towards us as if floating on air, wearing sarongs of such fine material and such warm colouring that their bodies are impossible to ignore despite the fact that they are as discreetly and modestly draped as devout Muslims. But you can't mask beauty and grace, Marlo, and my heart falls like a leaf circling in drift to the sand beneath the mango tree. Oh, the beauty of those smiles, the captivation of their languorous ease. Oh, mango sirens, how you gladden the heart.

Tell Grandma to stop huffing, Marlo. My job in the world is to observe beauty and honour it. It's a serious occupation. This attraction is what makes the world go around and creates little Marlos. How to notice the world's beauty and still honour Grandma, that's the trick, Marlo. And she's not really your grandma, but there're no grandchildren of her own yet so you'll have to do.

Where were we? Ah, yes, the magical mango tree, surrounded by broken toys, canine computer engineers and impossibly beautiful women. And art. This is an artist's community and would make Ubud look like a day in Altona. I've been to Ubud and was terrified by the number of people and the stench of sewer drains and piles of garbage in the street. But Ubud is the pinnacle, I was told, the ultimate Shangri-la of art, the oasis of the creative impulse. I was so alarmed I had to catch a bus and sit by a remote beach in the north of Bali. Ubud: artists' colony my eye.

I've got to catch the dogs so they can be sedated prior to surgery, so I follow a gorgeous woman in a sarong as she sings to the dogs in a treble so light that I faint and the dogs melt. 'Ice-cream, Chocolate, Battery,' she calls, and the dogs simper to her feet. What's the odd word among the dogs' names? Yes, old Battery. How did he miss out in the sweetness stakes? Not because he's a mad charging animal, he's as friendly and docile as any male is sure to become in this vicinity. But somehow he got called Battery, and everyone laughs when they say his name. The dog has developed a complex. Though he hides it well.

When all the dogs are recovering, I bring them to the rear of the house where there's a Rupert Bunny idyll. The old Rupert didn't work plastic bread bags and cordial bottles into his paintings: how could he, they weren't invented then. In those days we used things we could reuse, like glass and ... don't get me started on the modern world, Marlo, or we'll never get this story finished.

So I bring old Ice-cream back and they examine her stitches and the woman croons, 'Oh, Ice-cream, Ice-cream, you poor little dog.' What about me, I think, I had a tooth out once, don't I get a bit of a croon? Stop it, Grandpa, you're obsessed. Who said that? Was it you, Marlo, or your mother? Look, there's nothing wrong with loving women, as long as you keep it tidy. And you examine my life, and you'll note the extraordinary discretion and restraint I've shown! I've never been unfaithful. As long as you don't count the celebration of beauty as being unfaithful. Men can look, Marlo, but your grandma says it depends on *how* you look. I'd learn that look if I were you, my boy.

Anyway, back to Rupert Bunny. He's painted the deep green shade of the mango tree and the whole family reclined in it,

enjoying the breeze. One woman feeds her baby while combing her older daughter's hair. The man of the family, who makes
a point of rarely meeting my eye, has a tiny baby in his lap and
occasionally picks up one of its hands and kisses the fingers. He's
separating grass fibres that have come out of the dyeing tub. He
lays bundles of them carefully on an old blue tarp and then kisses
his baby's fingers or foot. He wears a pair of electric blue shorts
with plenty of electricity in them still, and in this company I can
understand that.

The beautiful woman, the *really* beautiful one, is making an
intricate table mat with a gradation of coloured grasses so fine you
have to look twice to see that the colour is not uniform. Or three
times if you want to sneak a look at her hands. Her old uncle sits
alone at the edge of the shade, on a car seat from a Hillman Minx
if I'm not very much mistaken. He's turned away from Rupert
Bunny's other subjects. Probably irascible. He's making a six-foot-
long crocodile out of charred strands of nobbly bark. The section
he's putting together looks like charred strands of nobbly bark but
the part he's finished looks like a bloody crocodile. Which reminds
me to apologise to you for biting your arm on the day you were
born and all the subsequent days and going, 'Look out, Marlo, a
crocodile's gunna get you.' Have you developed a fear of northern
salty streams, Marlo? I'm sorry, it looked like fun at the time. And
you were always kind enough to laugh.

One baby has been asleep on the concrete for the whole time
we've been here, but a dog sometimes checks to see if it's okay
by licking its bum crack. 'Cyclone,' the woman warns. Poor old
Cyclone, get blamed if the cat had kittens. One baby crawls away
on an adventure and finds an old sauce bottle. 'Lily, Lily,' she

croons to the child, who looks up at her mother with a face like a sunrise. As you would.

They all speak in Yolgnu and I recognise one word in fifty, but a voice is never raised except at Blackie, a dog that refuses to take its medicine. Even so, the call of 'Blackie, Blackie, Blackie, pup, pup' sounds to me like the sweet breath of angels.

During the course of the day I collect and return four dogs and always find an excuse to sit down and tickle a dog or remove a compact disc from a baby's mouth. Ah, Rupert, I think, paradise with bread bags and dirty mattresses. Although Rupert never painted black people. Maybe they never looked good in muslin. What do you think?

Everything is on the ground so everything becomes the colour of the ground. You see babies asleep with dogs on mattresses strewn with clothes and footy boots. And yet the babies are clean. The children's faces shine. No snotty noses here. Their clothes are bright and fresh. Who does the laundry? Where do they do the laundry?

Three girls sneak up to the operating table to watch the intestines being drawn out, edited and returned. They murmur and sigh, but only in sympathy with their dog. There's no shrieking or covering their faces. They've seen their uncle paint the intestines of animals a thousand times. They know where the bits are and what they do.

'This is the baby bag,' the vet says as he snips the sack. They murmur, 'Oh, Sheba.' No longer Queen. But they're neither dismayed nor shocked. The older girl shows her sister where the organ is located in her own body. They speak in language so I don't understand, but you only need to watch their faces to follow the conversation.

As the older girl explains the procedure, the sister looks up and her face is a beautiful sun. Well, we know where she gets that from. Her hair flies away in cool auburn flames and she is unbelievably, classically gorgeous.

The older girl's face is a study. She has heavier features, more like her father, almost sombre until she smiles and then you see an old-fashioned, austere beauty. Her skin is blue-black and it is the blue that shines when she smiles. Bewitching.

When we were young, my sister and I bought a painting for my mother of an Islander woman whose cheekbones shone green. The height of sophistication, it was at the time. My sister said it was art. This blue-black sister wears a spotlessly clean Footscray footy jumper. The middle sister, a vivid shirt dyed in the same tub as the grasses, if I'm not wrong. A rich, warm umber. Stunning against her skin.

There's a younger girl, who is just a ratbag, and she skips away after a dog with that hoppity-go-kick joy of the untroubled child; the feet dance and you wonder what would happen if some genius got 300 Yolngu kids together and taught them gymnastics and hurdles. Gold medals would fall like fruit from the trees. Beats pampering drug cheats and bar-room brawlers.

Alright, Marlo, I will apologise to the vast majority of Australia's hard-working Olympic athletes. Of course, their skill and honesty should be defended at every opportunity. But there is a black disc among the Olympic rings, isn't there? I'm hoping my country can leapfrog hatred. Javelin prejudice. Gold, gold, gold for Australia in the tolerance marathon over innumerable hurdles.

Is it the strangeness or the difference white Australians find most unsettling, or the effort required to tell one from the other?

Difference is black compared to white, clothing style compared to clothing style, four people in a house compared to twenty. Strangeness is that most Australians wouldn't be able to point to Maningrida on a map or say what language they speak there, even though it's in their own country. Difference is superficial but strangeness is deep inside the brain.

That's all, Marlo: I just want you to be a good Australian. It is what I hope for myself. Despite my irascibility.

RENE OF RAINBIRD CREEK

*R*ight bower. *On top of the left. And the ace. Good hand. Winning. What a nuisance.*

She sighed and hoped someone would go no trumps or misère. It wasn't that she didn't want to win – just not tonight. She was a bit nervy again. Didn't want to attract attention, even good-natured congratulations.

She loved card night, but sometimes she needed to hide a bit. Lie low. Like tonight. She knew by the breathiness at the base of her throat, the flutter. *Let me just sit here and listen to the talk, the scandalous stories, the retelling of impossible bedroom dramas, the breakfast barneys.*

And then she got the queen and the ten. Blimey.

The cards were flipped, the tricks fell, Roma finished a story about what he said and what she said: '... big time, and then he goes, Oh well, that's it then, and she goes, Yeah, and he goes, Right then, and ... Jesus, Rene, you had every trick. You lose points for that, calling six hearts and then winning the lot. Aren't you concentrating or something?'

Rene scratched at the edge of her beer coaster, and mercifully Kerry asked, 'So what'd she do then?'

'Nothin',' said Roma, 'he just left, packed everything in the ute and left.'

'Jesus.'

'Yeah.'

'She's better off.'

'Yeah.'

'You wouldn't think so, bawling her eyes out she is.'

'Is she?'

'Yeah, *desolate* she says ... wouldn't come to cards or nothin'.'

'Jesus.'

'Yeah.'

A man walked into the bar, a stranger, in a thick woollen jacket. They sized him up in one glance. Little pub like this, only stop on the highway in the middle of the hundred-plus-kilometre forest. Had to be a truckie. Heard the air brakes too.

He glanced at them, nodded – it was that sort of pub, too small not to acknowledge those already there – and stood for a moment with his back to the fire, a brace of wood-chopping trophies bristling from the mantel behind his shoulders. It wasn't rude to hog the fire for a while; almost everyone did at this time of year, even strangers. It was a magnet.

'Porterhouse is on special, love, if you want it,' Vera called from the bar, 'cause that silly Veronica didn't come tonight, mopin' about some man. You want it, love, with chips 'n' veggies?'

'Yeah.'

'Or salad?'

'Salad.'

Strewth, a man who ate salad. Still, it got rid of the porterhouse she'd cooked out of Monday-night habit.

'Where're you from?'

'Sydney.'

'Going to?'

'Melbourne.'

'Truckin'?'

'Yeah. Load of cattle.'

'Good-o then love, steak won't be long. Don't get mixed up with them girls though, they're ... voracious.'

All the voracious girls giggled, some even touching their hair or the top button of their card-playing blouse, the second best, satin, sort of.

He bought a pot of light beer. They noticed that. Responsible. He sat with his back to them and plucked at the pages of last week's *Forest Leaves:* old badminton results, desultory fishing reports, front page bagging the minister about criminal forest policy, crucifying the bush, again.

Vera brought his plate and an army of sauce bottles and condiments. He cut into the steak. Not very hot, but it'd been in the warmer for a while. The chips were good.

Rene wouldn't go to the bar to get her own drinks. Had to have company. Moral support. Usually Roma would go with her. Nothing bothered Roma. Anyone who wore men's work pants and a plaid shirt was obviously impervious to shame, but even though she wasn't as tough as she looked, she stuck by her mates, and she'd never let anyone pick on Rene.

The man watched the smaller woman. Neat. Nervy like a finch, but tidy in her poverty, if he wasn't mistaken. The clothes were Kmart for sure, but he could see they'd been chosen with care, kept clean, pressed, never washed with socks or towels.

He studied the profile of her face, recognised the history written there.

The cards were flipped, greeted with triumph or disdain, the stories slipping in between shuffles, but quieter now, not as bawdy, or as cruel.

A couple of men shouldered their way into the bar, bought their beers and set up a game of pool, acknowledging the women's comments with practised indifference.

'Geez, your bum looks big in those, Michael.'

'Got Eileen pregnant again, Rog?'

The click of the balls punctuated the flip of the cards.

Roma escorted Rene to the bar for the next round but veered off to the toilets. The man picked up his empty glass and casually took it to the bar and waited for Vera to fill it. Rene was pretending to pick up her drinks but her little hands were never going to get around four pots.

He turned to her with his back to Vera and said, so no one else could hear, 'You're Koorie, nah?'

She looked up, startled, the breath fluttering at the top of her throat. But she nodded.

'So am I. Where're your people from?'

'Don't know,' the little woman breathed.

'Don't know? So what's your name?'

'Arnold.'

'Arnold?'

'But me mum was a Kane.'

'Kane? And you don't know where they're from?'

'No.'

'Know anything about them?'

He heard the toilet door slam and knew Roma was returning, but she just leaned between them, scooped up three of the pots and carried them back to the card table, winking extravagantly to the girls. Well, he didn't seem a bad sort of bloke – and she could recognise bad sorts of blokes, had kicked plenty of them out. But bad blokes seldom ate salad. In her experience. Which wasn't small. Not small at all, quite often.

Rene kind of shrugged. She wasn't used to talking to men. She knew nothing about her family. 'But I've looked,' she told him. 'There was this book I saw in the mobile library.'

'And you looked under Kane and couldn't find anything?'

'No.'

'Did you spell it with a C or a K?'

'K, I've always spelt it with a K. That's what Mum said it was.'

Rene was twisting her pot on the bar towel, hoping Roma would come and rescue her, even glancing towards the table, but they all seemed oblivious.

'Did you look under C?'

'C?'

'For Cane.'

'Cane?'

'You're a Cane, I'd bet anything on it. Your grandmother and grandfather are heroes. Took on the government when they tried to kick the people off the mission. Your family's famous.'

Oh, no. Famous. How can I hide? Why doesn't Roma come and help me?

'I bet your family is looking for you. I'll tell you what, I'm coming back next week, next Monday it'll be – card night, isn't it? I'll find out for you if you like.'

He watched her face. Her lips moved a bit, and there was a sort of nod of assent. Or it could have been a jerky intake of breath.

'Well. I'll see you then. Next Monday.'

*   *   *

The cards fell, mostly from Rene's hands. 'Come on, Rene, you're not concentrating,' they yelled at her. 'Don't worry, he'll turn up, his type always does.'

His type. She tried to get the cards into suits but kept fumbling them.

'You trying to advertise that ace, Rene?'

But eventually they heard the air brakes.

'Your shout, Rene,' Roma called, even though everyone knew it was Kerry's. Roma stood up and handed Rene her purse. 'Time to let the moths out, darl.' She grinned. Well, Roma thought of it as her grin. Dogs put their tails between their legs.

Roma escorted Rene to the bar and left her there just as the man opened the door. Like a lot of big women, Roma's timing was pretty good. She was light on her feet. Surprisingly delicate. Delicate in dungarees.

He nodded at Rene, bought his beer.

'Porterhouse, darl?' Vera called. 'Make you a fresh one this week, Veronica's stopped sookin'.'

'Thanks.'

Vera bustled off to the other end of the bar. She was loud but not stupid. They all liked Rene. Protected her. As you do the smallest in the litter.

'Cane, alright,' he said, taking a sip from his glass. 'Irene Cane.'

'Irene?'

'Yes, Rene, I for Irene. You never knew?'

'No.'

'Your mum never said?'

'The home said she died when I was ten. Only saw her a few times.'

'Rene, she died three years ago. They were bullshittin' ya, the home.'

Rene froze, clutching her purse. Roma came up and took it from her hands, plucked a note, slapped it on the bar and returned to the cards, which were stalled, waiting, even the gossip abbreviated. Hard to talk when you were listening so hard.

'Those homes are full of shit, Rene. I was in one too. I saw it in you straightaway. I'm sorry about your mum, but they do that to you. Lie. Lie through their teeth. For your own good. So that you don't know who you are. And you're famous, Rene.'

She glanced at him in panic.

'You must have known, Rene, you're so dark.'

Her lips went to move but only kind of wriggled.

'Your family fought the government. They were heroes. Still are. Your aunty is a big shot in Canberra. Got 'em all bluffed, she has. Real tough cookie. Gotta be, or they'd crush her like an ant. Would you like to meet her? Your family? I could take you up there if you like. In the truck.' He put his hand in his pocket and withdrew a crumpled note and some coins. 'Buy you a drink, Rene?'

Roma saw the hand go in the pocket and come out with the money. No wallet, she thought, poor as ... poor as a half-black truck driver. Still, he was a decent poor half-black truck driver. Decent, she could tell that. Stood out like a beacon. Not her type. She liked 'em dangerous. Stupid bitch she was. Dangerous and big enough to throw her across the room. And some of them did. Even her, Big Roma. Still ...

'What do you say? I've got a house in Liverpool. Me uncle's, really. He'd set up a room for you while you had a look around and then I could bring you back next week if you wanted.'

Wanted. She'd never dared *want*.

'They know about you, Rene. Your family. Never knew what happened to you. Your sister went looking for you but the home said they didn't know where you were.'

'Sister?' Rene stared up into the man's eyes for the first time.

'Yeah, sister, you've got a sister. Two. They cried when I told them.'

So did Rene. Right there, couldn't help it, bubbling like a brook. Plopping fat tears onto the bar towel so that Vera plumped the plate of steak down on the bar with two beers and scuttled off. 'Strewth, Rene's cryin'. Something's up.'

'Who are you?' It was Roma. Big and bustling, hoping she hadn't made a huge mistake.

'Kevin Murray. I'm her cousin, sort of.'

'Cousin!'

Rene was too damp to gasp.

'So that means you can make her cry, *sort of?*'

'I know her family. I know her sisters.'

'Sisters,' Roma said, glaring.

'Yes, she's got a whole family looking for her. Koorie family.'

'Don't take us for mugs, Kevin, it's obvious what she is, but she's our mate, and you hurt her and *The Texas Chainsaw Massacre*'ll be nothin' on what we do to you. But look, she's just won the raffle jackpot.'

'What jackpot?' Vera asked.

'*The* jackpot, you stupid fat bitch, the Monday $100 jackpot.'

'Oh yes,' Vera tried to perk up and follow the hint, 'number 49 Blue.' She handed over the $100, hoping the other girls would cough up part of it. Sort of like a dowry or something. Even if he was a sort of cousin.

Roma put her shoulder between Rene and Kevin. 'Hurt her and we'll kill you,' she muttered. 'I'll kill you. No funny business. She's got a family, you take her to her family and bring her back. And after that she can decide. But a new family – it takes thinking about. Alright?'

Kevin didn't reply. He wasn't about to be intimidated by bluster. He knew what he knew and he'd do what he'd always done. What he thought was best. He didn't need to be lectured. He stared her down. Or tried to. But she'd met enough truck drivers not to shift her gaze.

'She doesn't need any more bad luck.'

Roma talked as if Rene wasn't there.

'This is *good* luck, she's got a family, sisters. With our people that's good luck.'

Roma just looked at him. He didn't need to tell her about *his* people. Small bush mill towns. Plenty of *his* genes spread around those places. Paid not to look too close, to ignore unexplainable suntans. Not to ask too many questions. Even about your own family. But sisters. That was different. Rene had sisters.

Roma steered Rene back to the table and they reacquainted themselves with their cards.

'Don't mind Roma – what's your name?' said Vera.

'Kevin.'

'Look, Kevin,' Vera went on, 'don't mind her, she's too big for her boots, and she's got bloody big boots, but she's also got —'

'A heart of gold?'

'Well, what's wrong with that? She's only lookin' after her mate. Rainbird's a small town, Kevin, we look out for each other, especially the women. And Rene's been ripped off a few times.'

'I'm her cousin.'

'So you say, after drivin' a truck up to the pub after dark, but she's *our* mate.'

'I know that, and I *am* her cousin.'

'Good. And Kevin, your truck plate is RA1390 and your CB is 863030. We only know who you say you are, but we know where to find you … And you won't need another drink if you're driving to Sydney.'

'Canberra.'

'Well, Canberra then. I suppose someone has to go there.'

*   *   *

'They threatened to kill me,' he said.

Rene just looked down the tunnel of light that sucked them through the forest. She wished she hadn't got into the truck. She clutched her purse, couldn't see a place to put it. He might be wrong. They mightn't be her sisters, and if they were they mightn't like her.

She was better off back in the bush. Knew where the teapot was. Fed the birds at the back step. Watched the quiz shows, amazed by the answers. Played cards on Monday. Spent pocket money from part-time at the post office. Knew the routine, knew where she was, where she belonged, safe at last. What was she doing in the truck?

With a stranger? A cousin she didn't know. He might be wrong. Easy for him to say he knew all the answers, but if he was wrong, think of the upset, the ... problems.

'Put your purse in the glovebox, Rene. Listen, your grandmother wrote to the government and said they couldn't just turn around and give the mission to the farmers. It was her home, she told them, and was given to her people by the Queen. That's what she told them. Told them they'd have to carry her out. But she was smart too, told 'em she'd seen the original document, where it said while the people are still alive and want to live there the place was theirs. She could read and write, see, very smart woman.

'They tried to say that because she was living with a man who wasn't her husband she'd have to go. She said that's *your* rules, not *our* rules, and *your* document says nothin' about who has to live with who. She could quote them letter and verse, Rene, she was a smart woman, a hero, and if you weren't able to take your place in that family, it'd be a crime. Like, they'd been successful at last. Got what your grandmother had stopped them from getting. That's all I thought, Rene, I thought you should know and your sisters should know and we should know, all the rest of your family, *we'd* know that they hadn't won again. That's all. I didn't mean to upset you.'

She looked down the tunnel veering through the rushing trees.

'You're famous, Rene. We need you.'

My teapot, my flowers. The thrush won't get his cheese. Who'll be a millionaire next?

'It doesn't work out, tell my uncle, he'll get you back home, he's the best man alive. He's your uncle too, sort of. He'll get you home. Or I can drive you next week.'

Sisters and uncles was one thing, but that thrush needed her, sang to her. What would happen to the thrush? It might think she'd deserted it, never given it another thought.

'Can I …' she began. 'Can I ring Roma on that thing' – she indicated the CB radio – 'and see if she'll feed my bird?'

SOLDIER GOES
TO GROUND

It was a paddy field that had been slurped into mush, like a huge plate of cereal. And they were firing at him. He didn't want to be killed. He didn't want to feel the scorch of hot metal rip through his tissues. As he ran, he could imagine the lead searching to plunge a hole through his back. His spine tingled as he slushed through the mud and blasted harvest.

There was a lump, a sodden thing, and he fell beside it, hiding his head. He panted into his arm, his body sinking into the sour mud. The firing continued, but nothing found a cave of flesh, at least not his flesh. He opened his eyes and saw that his shelter wore a uniform, the same uniform, and that the intestines were beginning to stray from beneath the jacket. They were a puzzle, a mystery, an organic jigsaw.

He couldn't be sick. He couldn't be sad. He had his own warm sac of tubes to protect from the blazing hounds of the air. What were they firing at? He seemed to have been here for hours. Surely the others were all gone, or dead, like this fallen lump he was hiding behind. He dared not lift his head. Perhaps they assumed he was dead. He let his face sink deeper into the slush, wishing that the mud would embrace him, take him into its arms and protect him.

'G'day.' Silence punctuated by bursts of fire. 'Rather be at Lorne, meself.'

Who spoke? Involuntarily, he lifted his head an inch and swivelled his eyes to look around. No one, only the corpse. And then he saw the eyes looking at him.

'Give you a fright, did I? You'd better stick your head down again, mate. You can stay here until it stops. I don't think I'm going anywhere.'

His eyes slewed to the side to look at the mess of gut seeping from beneath the jacket, and he felt ashamed of the glance, but the corpse had seen the direction of his gaze.

'I know. I tried to put it back, but I can't move anymore. I can't even feel it anymore. Like a bad dream, except it's not, is it?'

'Can I do —'

'No, I don't think so.' The dead and living gazed at each other across eight inches of mud.

'There is one thing you can do for me, in return for a bit of shelter.' A sick green smile stretched the facial muscles of the spoilt soldier. 'There's something in my top pocket, and I want you to give it to someone in Melbourne.'

A sodden silence.

'Take it for me.'

The living soldier watched in dismay as a bead of moisture fled the cheek of the face that was taking on the texture of an old sago pudding.

'Give it to a girl who lives at 46 Pacific Street, Brunswick. Sue.'

The breath was still stirring the puddle between their faces, but the eyes had closed. The lips parted jerkily once more, but no sound came, and the pool of slush became still.

He stared for an age at the white-green mask, before he saw his fingers grappling with the button of the top pocket. These fingers disappeared and withdrew a shell, a frail pink shell. In acres of slop and screaming air, two fingers held a perfect shell.

Pacific Street. Pacific Street. Forty? Forty-eight? Forty-six.

Brunswick. Brunswick. In the hardly credible world away from this rice bowl, there was Brunswick, a casual half-hour drive from his own home.

The sky began to turn an acrid yellow as sunset became soured with the smoke of shellfire and marsh haze. The last shots were fired, and two pucked into the back of the sheltering corpse and jerked it like a baker might casually thump a bag of flour. A dull, thick sound.

Shell, shells. Shell, shells. He slunk away from the curdling sack of guts, bearing with him the shell. An eye for an eye. A shell for a shell.

*　　*　　*

Life was best lived in a daze. Not a stupor, but a coma of the softer parts of the mind. The bits for running, drinking and eating could continue unimpaired, while the other senses crouched away from the bodies falling or bleeding, the gaping faces of mothers and children, the flames, the ruined fields, the spoilt soldiers in threshed fields of grain. Discarded sacks of life. As wasteful and careless as a bag of kittens in a sewer.

But he ran and hid, drank and ate, and nothing punctured his frail consciousness, and nothing pierced his warm bag of flesh, until one day he saw a boy's face appear between leaves.

There was a flash, and he almost saw it coming for his leg. The child was terrified and had hardly aimed at all. But ten others aimed at the boy, and his pouch of life was penetrated and then left to bloat like a cow – or a calf.

He watched in amazement from starchy sheets as infection grew and the sag-eyed doctors stood around, lifting the sheet to look at his leg, to glance at each other, and finally to send him home.

And to be sure, there was a bit missing out of his leg, but it healed perfectly. The boy in the bushes had sent him a ticket for home and paid for it. Dearly.

*   *   *

Pacific Street, Brunswick. He stepped from the car and walked in suburban-street sunshine to the terrace with '46' screwed to the mortar. The door knocked hollow. It opened and a girl looked out at him inquiringly.

'Does Sue live here?'

'Yes, she's inside. I'm Brenda. Come in.'

Brenda turned and sashayed into the kitchen. 'Suzanne, there's a man to see you.'

'Hullo. I, I knew a friend of yours. Could I speak to you privately?'

Brenda whistled. 'Wow, what a smoothie!'

She saw his eyes as she spoke, and left the room swiftly.

'I was in Penang and I met this man, and he gave me your address and a present for you, and he died before he could say . . . His name was Ken Simpson.'

Suzanne drew on a cigarette and stared at the man before her. She pressed the butt into an ashtray. 'Look, oh look, I'm sorry, but I only moved here two months ago. The other girl before me, she was called Sue. I'm Suzanne. Sue's gone to Sydney with – I'm really sorry. Look, sit down and I'll get you a cup of coffee.'

She clanked the kettle onto the stove and tossed spoons of coffee into mugs. 'Was he a friend of yours?'

The soldier looked up from his hands. 'No, well, I'd only just met him.'

She held a cup of coffee towards him. 'Was that the present?' she asked as she nodded towards the shell.

'Yes, he didn't say what …'

They drank the silence from their coffee cups and, though his face was averted, she could tell he was crying, twisting the shell in his hands. He turned to her. 'I'm sorry, it's not the shell or anything. I hardly, I only knew him for a few minutes, but for the first time –'

She'd seen enough Rock Hudson films to know that this is what soldiers do when they come home. And there is always a Florence Nightingale to apply the soft hand and soothing words. 'Look, we're having a party here tonight. Why don't you stay and join in?'

Brenda entered the room and saw the soldier looking crumpled and Suzanne's hand on his shoulder. Suzanne glanced at her friend. 'This man, he knew one of Sue's boyfriends, it seems, and came to give her a present. We haven't even got her Sydney address, have we? What was that Stewart fella's name? We might be able to look that up in the phone book. Anyway, I've invited him,' Suzanne nodded to indicate the soldier, 'to the party.'

She brought him wine and cheeses while she tidied the house and made plates of food. He watched through the window the last sun on terrace walls turning the street into a flat façade. She filled his wineglass again and he allowed himself to drop behind the aquarium, with its lonely goldfish. People came and went around him. The party spread and grew, dividing carefully around his chair.

The music washed up against the glass in front of his face, and the dancers were like weeds moving in the water.

'Hey mate, this yours?' A shell was held over his face, and he reached up from the deep and took it, slipping it into his pocket.

I'd rather be in Lorne.

He woke with sun creeping across his eyes, and he stared at the window, waiting to realise where he was.

Pacific Street, 46, Brunswick.

There was a body behind him, its arm flung across his neck. He reached back and touched the skin. Warm. His hand followed the curve of hip and thigh, and he turned his head. The eye was looking at him. 'Sleep?'

'Must have.'

She reached across him and picked up the shell from a table and held it for him to see. 'I saved your shell. You started yelling a bit.'

'Did I?'

'Mmmm. About Lorne. If you keep it up, they might make you mayor.' She ran a hand round the scoop of his waist and over his belly, and the tingling of his vulnerability was like pain. Sharp as blades.

*   *   *

'Dearly beloved,' the minister half-yelled into the wind. This was the first time he had heard the soldier of shelter's name. The family looked at him, but after the service turned to shepherd the mother from the grave. He was left in the wind and the sour smell of clay. His coat flapped at his legs and blew hair back from his face. He leant forward and dropped the shell into the grave.

'Friend of yours, son?'

His heart leapt. People were forever creeping up and talking at him. His heart slowed down and he turned to see the man with the spade. 'Yes, a friend.'

'Very sorry, mate.' The shoveller was waiting to shovel.

At the iron gates of the cemetery he pushed his hands into his pockets, and the fingers involuntarily searched the linings before he turned his eyes to the street.

'Bunch of flowers, sir?'

Christ! He pushed money at her before she could speak again. He pressed the marigolds to his stomach and hurried up the street.

*   *   *

'Flowers!' she said, and he held them out to her. She brought the yellow and gold to her face and looked at him, wondering about the next move, the next word. The trip wires and triggers, shelters and tombs. Neither of them spoke across the marigolds.

THE HEADLESS HORSEMAN OF THE DRUMMER

for Uncle Herb and Uncle Sandy ... at work

D id you ever see him?

Oh, yes, dozens of times, me and the others ... well, not see him, but we knew he was there. I'd never go over that mountain at night. Still won't. Rather stay at the bottom, in someone's house. Go on next morning. Sometimes used to stay with them, Mc something ...

McArthurs.

Yeah, that mob. Had this little house —

Bit of a walkway across that swampy flat.

Near the mill.

Back of the mill. They had that little —

Yeah, poor thing. Wonder whatever happened to her.

Up in Eden last time I heard, livin' with that lady.

That's right, her aunt.

Cousin. Haunty Clarrie.

Yeah. Got the house behind ...

Stewarts'.

Yeah, they ever sell that?

The old Valiant wagon, nah.

Remember them days.

The picnics.

The funerals.

Smugglin' the dead.

That poor old Valiant.

Yeah, I'd only need to look at that old —

Yeah, it'd all come back, eh.

Remember them old ten-gallon kero tins?

Cut 'em down an' make buckets.

Bath fa' the baby ...

Cut it flat, tin for the roof.

Yeah. I was talkin' to old Granny Hagnes, Verna's mum.

In the home.

Yeah. She was down in the dumps, like. I was tryin' to cheer her up, type of thing.

Yeah.

Talk about them bean pickin' days.

On the river.

All the corn ...

An' peas ...

Yeah, an' I was talkin' about this one or the other, just fishin', ya know, an' then I mentioned them tins, sort of in passin', an' she goes, Honey. What, I said. They was honey tins, the old girl goes, golden syrup an' the like.

Cocky's delight.

Yeah, get 'em from down the tip.

Cut 'em down.

Wire handle.

Yeah, boil up the clothes.

Leg of roo.

Wash the dog.

Chainsaw parts.

Carbies.

Pippis.

Yeah, remember them pippis, eh.

Them days down at Bemm.

Chuck the pippis in, bit of salt water.

Clean 'em out.

Rid of all that grit.

Yeah.

Next mornin', boil 'em up.

Heat 'em.

Yeah.

Boilin's too hard.

Make 'em tough.

Yeah, unless you was gunna curry 'em.

Yeah.

Them little square tins of curry powder.

Yeah. Oblong.

Keen's.

Yeah.

Aunty Darly, the one with the —

Yeah, how is the old girl?

Still up in Shep.

Yeah, all this time.

She'd have to be ...

Eighty.

Easy.

Yeah.

Well, she was the one for the curry.

Yeah.

She'd curry ya boots if ya left 'em by the fire.

And they'd taste alright.

Yeah.

They was good days, eh.

Work hard.

Work.

Like bloody slaves.

Were slaves.

But somehow ...

Yeah.

We was our own boss, a bit.

Yeah.

Nights by the fire.

Singin'.

Remember Handy Tappy an' his—

Yeah.

Play good, that old man.

Play anything.

Too right, ya know one night I heard him play that ...

'Rhapsody in Blue'.

Yeah. How can you play that on guitar? I make my livin' playin' the bloody thing an' I never been able to work out how he done that.

Yeah.

All them classical people he'd do.

Yeah. Porter.

An' Harmstong.

Yeah, the old Satch. Used ta love him. Sing like him too.

Yeah.

An' what's his name ... Fella with all the hair ...

Yeah.

Black man.

Yeah.

Could do him a treat.

He died up ...

Yeah.

Now he *did* see the horseman.

Dooligas.

Yeah.

Up on that other mountain.

Yeah, Gooliga.

He did see that fella.

Old Handy, eh.

Yeah.

Wouldn't ya love to sit by the fire an' listen to him play?

Yeah.

An' them Carters an' Mumblers.

An' Roses.

Yeah, the Rose boys.

On the leaf.

An' mouth organ.

Oh, them nights.

Yeah.

Out by the river.

Remember that night ...

Yeah, the Goonitch bird come.

Yeah.

Old lady ...

Pressie.

Yeah, she got all us kids chuckin' stones an' makin' a racket.
Get that bird outa here. She'd —

Stick her hands over her face.

Apron an' all.

Get that bird outa here, it'll be the death of me.

Chuckin' rocks.

Sticks.

Hanything.

That one with the big white face.

Yeah.

Goonitch.

They was real frightened, eh, them old people.

Terrified. Screamin'.

An' cryin'.

Get that bird!

Well, I am too.

Remember we was campin' with old uncle ...

Thomas.

An' we heard that bird, an' he goes, come on you fellas, we're
gettin' ...

Yeah.

Pack up camp.

We was only little.

Yeah. Come on, we're goin'.

Yeah.

Remember old Uncle Muns.

Hammon.

Yeah. Remember that thing he did with the wattle?

Old fellas told me.

He showed me one day. Not showed me, just did it so I could see.

The billy.

Yeah. He'd cut around the elbow of a wattle. Like this, see, an'
then he'd prize it off with a stick ...

Yeah.

An' put it on the fire with water an' it'd boil.

Ol' fellas told me.

Ol' Muns.

Spirit Man.

An' his dogs.

Three of them.

An' the bike.

Yeah, wouldn't ride it, just walk beside it.

Coast down the hills a bit. I seen him do that once when I was
rabittin' with ol' Huncle Col.

Just coast down the hill.

With them dogs.

One in front.

One beside him.

An' one at the back.

Yeah.

Now *he* saw the horseman, too.

Huncle Col?

Yeah. He saw him an' he wasn't a man ta get scared.

No.

But the hair stood up on the back of his neck an' cold water was runnin' down his back. Sweat, like.

Yeah.

An' he was lookin' about. Knew he was there somewhere. Just froze.

I never go over that mountain at night.

Me neither.

Stay with them, Macs.

McArthurs.

Yeah. In that little house.

By the swamp.

Yeah.

You know that ol' Granny Hagnes? It was like that with her. I don't know nothin' about them old days, she'd go, an' I just mentioned them tins an' off she goes. Honey, she says, an' that was it.

Yeah.

An' just as I was goin', feelin' pretty pleased to have revved the old girl up, she goes, them Stewarts, they ever sell that Valiant? Don't know, Aunt, I goes, an' I didn't, which is why I asked you just before. An' she looks at me an' goes, well, that's how I want to go. In that Valiant.

Yeah.

So, I said, alright Granny, I'll ask that ol' Huncle Erb. Which I just done.

So she can go in style.

Like the old people.

She'd like that.

COFFINS

I could hear them making the box. Chipboard and staples. They measured me first, but it was only a gesture; they'd already guessed what they'd need.

Ca-lick, ca-lick, ca-lick, the tiny detonations of the staples. I saw the black paint come out, could smell it, heard the desultory slap of the brush, the *snip, snip, screer* of the shears cutting the black cloth to size. *Screer, snip, snip, screer. Ca-lick, ca-lick, ca-lick.*

It was darker than I'd expected, and unnerving hearing the mourners breathing, clearing their throats behind balled fists. For silence and repose. I saw their hands clutching the side of the open coffin. Fingers drumming, waiting, impatient; a stage silence. Disconcerting to look up to see the undersides of their fingernails and chins. And I saw the ring on a tense finger and knew who owned that hand. An injured bird, jittery, startled into flicking its wings like fans held by nervous ladies. Knew that hand would never again touch the beaver-pelt heads of three of her sons. Can you believe such a loss, how God spaced it to attenuate the pain?

What did I have to whinge about? I stared at that hand and resolved to be still, a good, unremarkable corpse, do nothing to remind her and have to meet her eye. But of course everything reminded her. Seen three coffins, seen them all.

I lay still and listened to some dreary hymn that I would never have chosen. But then I heard a tune I did recognise, although I didn't choose that either, but knew that this cued the beginning of the end.

I will follow him, follow him wherever he may go. There isn't a mountain too high, an ocean so wide it can keep, keep me away, away from his love.

They were wheeling my box and singing as we travelled up the aisle to André bloody Rieu.

Near the pulpit, they shuffled the box into position. The trolley wheels squeaked; the priest took possession of the apex and sighed. Straining my gaze backwards, I could see his knuckles, hear his boredom in every breath.

'Here we go, cock,' he whispered to me as André let fly with a final crescendo of a thousand strings dribbling with golden syrup. Cocky's delight. 'Here we go.'

'Dearly beloved,' the priest intoned, his voice rising in portent and volume, shrouding his tedium in pomp, deluding all except me, who could look up his nose and see the flaring of his nostrils and the whiffle of disdain in the hairs that clustered there like fishing flies. 'We are gathered here today to celebrate the life ...' and so on and so forth; the practised intonation of his voice, pacing, timing the words until he hit his cue like a hammer on a coffin nail.

And on that cue André allowed a beat and then came in double time.

I love him, I love him, I love him, and where he goes I'll follow, I'll follow, I'll follow.

Even though strings and drums were belting and wailing, I could hear the ruffle of efficient hands as they drew away my shroud and felt certain I could reclaim the *snip, snip, screer* as the material parted to the honed jaws of the shears.

Three beats, four beats, five beats, six beats, seven beats, eight beats and the padded sticks hit the pig skin and a chord ripped from the bass drum and I sat up in my box and began combing my hair. I recognised individual gasps and laughter, yep, performing for my friends to the end.

And so, some time later, when my favourite aunt invited me to watch two entire André Rieu concerts on a double DVD Easter special, I swallowed my pride and did as I was bid. Yes, I did as I was bid.

I loved my aunt – loved her for her goodness and wicked humour and because I couldn't look at her without remembering my father and how they used to clown in pantomime together. So at what point did she lose Roy Rene and Groucho Marx and find André Rieu?

I was struggling with my face. My eyes were trying to snuggle up in my beard and then I heard, *I love him, I love him, I love him, and where he goes . . .*

Wide awake, eyes rescued from the thickets, staring at the screen, confused by the reluctant resurrection from sleep and panicked by my cue music. André Bloody Rieu.

I survived the double DVD. Only just. Touch and go. Heroic.

I was named to honour my uncle who died in the Coral Sea so that General McArthur could return. I measured my valour in surviving the strings against my uncle's drowning beneath a toppled refrigerator. I thought I was in the same tent. But I would only win the Pacific Star because I loved my aunt.

And then it was a stream of cousins and children of cousins because vaudeville aunt had died. Only so often you can trapeze without the safety net.

It's a lie about the stream of cousins because there were several childless aunts, she being one of them, too busy in the footlights, and there was my uncle underneath the frij in the Coral Sea so that General Mc . . .

They'd burnt her into dust because that's what she wanted, a bit of flame and smoke, a bit of theatre, good lights, props.

I loved her, so I stood up and said I loved her and told the story of the big family who lived in a shoe and their mother who didn't know what to do. Perhaps because she knew she was a bit black. Or maybe she didn't; maybe I just expected her to activate curiosity. But she probably thought the world wasn't ready for slapstick magic. She was right.

Uncle was crying, as he should, because he loved the clown aunt with all his soul, and like his beloved's mother didn't know what to do.

And after all the PowerPoint of my aunt in pantomime drag – drover, Mother Christmas, Easter bunny, showgirl, Peter Pan – I was in tears and desperately trying to repair myself in time to help my cousin from the pew because she'd developed a crook knee somewhere in the last thirty years. I was flicking tears off my cheeks as if combing a troublesome beard, but a beard never really gives trouble, except to those who have to look at bread and soup trapped in its maze.

I was thinking, *Lift cousin Judy by the elbow, amazing that no one thought to call a son Punch, and ease her around . . .*

And there it was: the music. André Bloody Rieu. They were

going to finish with André. I was expected to guide a toppling cousin as a thousand strings shrieked and a million voices yodelled, *I love him, I love him, I love him* ...

Funny woman, my aunt. Saved the best joke for the end.

DAWN

You are perfect for this story. I will never meet you.

When I wake at night I am almost always turned to the right, turned to the night, a great field of stars before me. At this time of the year there is Corona Australis and another constellation arranged in a deep V. I don't know its name. I could look up what the Greeks or British decided to call it but I am neither Greek nor British, so I am happy to watch it rise away from me until, on my last observation, just before dawn, it has gone.

Yambulla rests his jaw on the bed and begs me to acknowledge that it is almost a new day and he is here. I rub the skin and fur of his eyebrows, jaw and ears to feel the bone beneath. This tells us that we are both alive and he can return to his bed until the sun has truly risen.

I turn away from the sky to watch her. She is just a nest of hair, a gorgeous silver scramble. The cover is drawn up so far as to hide her almost completely. I sneak the cover down so I can see her sleeping eyes. She murmurs, so I stop and watch. Her hair never went grey but sedately transmuted into a silver-gold. I lift a strand away from her eyes and she murmurs again, so again I watch and wait like a thief.

She moves, curving in closer to my chest. I feel her breast slip against me. Do you see why I am telling you this? It would be impossible to tell anyone else. Something deep within me caves as if a vacuum has been created every time I feel the slip of that sensuous weight.

When she makes the small animal alignments to bring her flesh more roundly to mine I restrain the doona so that it slips from her shoulder. She murmurs an objection. Always. But as always I put my hand there to cup the round of her shoulder, and she sighs, satisfied by the return of warmth. Her breath is warm and bodily.

I can see her throat now, and her lips, and if I am careful I can pass a hand across her brow and she will allow it, turn her face to the plane of my hand. This is illicit, salacious. I might look at her lips in the beige light of creeping dawn, but I cannot touch. One finger there and she will squirm and bring an irritated hand to her mouth, rubbing fractiously. I must not touch if my sin is to advance. I can look and linger, but that is all.

Her cheekbone is high and beautiful. My finger can ride that blade and a smile might crimp the edges of her lips. That is permitted so long as I return to the shoulder frequently enough to keep it warm. Otherwise she will draw the covers over herself and it will be over. Carefully, slowly, indecently, is the rule.

The wattlebirds have heard the kookaburra and so it is deemed to be dawn. The nightjar might be allowed one or two more freakish ululations, but the night heron leaves after one final *kwok*. The frog in the ferns has more loosely defined rules and will continue at his leisure or pleasure. It's hard to know about frogs, especially those so ridiculously named as the pobblebonk.

But in this light, a pinkish yellow like a new peach where it is caught by the sun, I can clearly see the skin of her face, and I don't know when I first noticed the new splashes of colour. They are uneven blurs, the colour of spilt tea on a napkin. She is tawny beneath my fingers. I press with the ball of muscle above my thumb and she mumbles, reassured. I may continue to stroke and smooth and stare.

I might slide a curved hand over her shoulder and down the gorgeous rise of her arm, and this action can cause the cover to slip a fraction and reveal the wonderful bulb of her breast. She would allow me to slip my fingers beneath it and cup, but then it would be over. The grey eyes would flick open and she would smile, but it would be over. Too soon.

I bring the doona higher on her shoulder and she turns into its warmth, murmuring again, but I wait until the breath puffs evenly from her lips in this sleep so girlishly simple.

I may let a finger slide into the cup below the shoulder blade and smooth the skin as it rises to her throat. I am allowed many liberties, but I must not touch the piece of bone that now lies across the rest of the blade where Mrs Whitlam broke it. Mrs Whitlam is a horse. Big and brave and beautiful, but scared of sudden wallabies and suspicious fence posts. Makes her shy.

So don't touch that bone. It would be over. She presses in closer to me and her breasts slide heavily against me. A thigh rises over mine and she squirms again, adjusting, moulding herself to me, fidgeting this limb and that, this foot against that, settling. It is not over yet. Her breath puffs evenly and I can see her lips pout at each slight eruption of air that forces between them. This is something only a wanton boy would admit to watching.

The lyrebird thinks that it is now time. To sing. Other people's songs. The silver-blonde woman is responsive to the bird and she opens her eyes, as grey and warm as the breast of a shrike-thrush, and asks me for the time. Not to know the time, but to know if she has another half-hour. I tell her whatever time it is that would assure her she has another half-hour to sleep, to merge. Her arm circles my waist and she presses her face to my neck. It is scandalous, the liberties I take with the truth to ensure this happens.

Now I can stroke her more boldly, rub the skin of her forehead, smoothing the wrinkles there. This is a beautifully moulded bone, and tawny with the new dabs of fawn.

I do not cry at my good fortune. I am used to it. Resigned. To the glory of her.

I draw a finger across the rise of her cheek, and at this late hour may smooth a line to the corner of her mouth. My hand slips down and cups her breast. The brow creases but I am out of control and caress the curve of her waist and the sweep where it careens across the smooth arch of her hip.

I remember the night before, when we watched a film. She was wearing shorts and she swung her legs imperiously into my lap. No words. It was expected I would stroke her feet. Some buckled toes, a craggy nail or two, but smooth, curved feet, strokeable feet. Yambulla grunted and moved to the end of the couch, resigned to the fact that all the affection tonight would be for her, not him.

And I found myself holding the long, loose muscle of her calf and then releasing, to let it fall into the curve of my palm. I couldn't remember doing this before, but it was delicious. Another illicit activity to savour. In this golden light my hand rests on the outside of her thigh, remembering the gentle slap of that calf muscle but unable to reach it now without terminal ruction of the dawn ceremony. The hand muses there, thrall to memory.

Now that the wattlebird is *catcher-catcher-catcher*ing and the wonga pigeons are ratcheting around on the verandah like clock-work toys, it is truly day, and she stirs and flings the doona from her, rising on one elbow to survey the day, and I am finally, cor-ruptly, allowed her full survey. She will permit me to press my face into her breasts, though not to take the nipple between my lips. Too early. Too licentious. But I do allow my hand the full liberty of swimming across her body, her curves, and finally to joggle that calf muscle, to feel the loose slap of it.

So there you are, stranger; it is dawn and you are the only per-son who will hear this story, for it is forbidden.

CULTURELINES

HERE IS A STORY I'D LIKE YOU TO TELL TO THAT OLD MAN

Dear Wanjiku,

Here is a story I'd like you to tell to that old man.

One day I cleaned a fish at the jetty on the Jinoor River (Genoa if you believe white men) and I looked around for my brother the pelican, but he must have been fishing somewhere else or snoozing on a tree trunk washed up by the last flood.

It wasn't a big flood, but because there hadn't been one for over a year there was plenty of fallen timber to wash into the stream and deposit on a sandbank.

He might be camped on one of those limed limbs, his beak swivelled over his shoulder and tucked into the feathers of his back. We are a similar age, the two of us, and he sees us as cousins, and if I'm drinking beer on the jetty at dusk he will often land on the old timber deck and walk up to me, speaking in his guttural way and settling beside me.

He's not looking for food because he knows I fish at dawn, and at this hour I rarely have rods or nets. No, he's not completely craven, he's simply after conversation and companionship with an equal, although the idea of equality may be mine. I talk to Baroongooba in the old language about the beauty of the sunset and the day's activity along the river. His eye, rimmed with a cere exactly the same colour as a vibrant yolk, hardly leaves my face when I speak and mine, even more rarely, leaves his.

But on this day he was somewhere else, dozing on a sandbar like an old marooned galleon awaiting the ship breakers, or perhaps his family of five were engaged in a tactical fishing operation with the little black cormorants. I imagined them working in strategic synchrony. Napoleon would have admired the inevitability of their success.

One day last autumn I was looking for orchids with my wife. We left the boat tied to a log and climbed the ridge to find the spider orchids that grow in the shallow, shaley soil on its crest. As we returned to the boat a small armada of pelicans landed at the entrance of the muddy inlet and sailed serenely into the embayment. There was nothing casual about their deliberation.

They fanned out in a line fifteen metres apart, and when fifty metres from the far bank, they waited and took up position like a platoon of panzers. Baroongooba, the pelican, looked at me briefly as if to say, Watch this, and then he tilted his head to look at the sky before turning his attention back to the far shore.

Suddenly there was a noise like a hundred scarves being waved. It wasn't loud but you noticed it because it was so distinctive, and it got closer and closer, and then a squadron of the little black cormorants veered into the bay in tight formation perhaps ten metres from the surface. It surprised us because they were almost at our eye level as we climbed back onto the boat.

We were like generals on a safe and distant hill overlooking the battle because that is in fact what it was. The cormorants planed in across the heads of the pelicans and in perfect series from the right they plunged into the water like missiles. The effect was like a well-aimed cannonade, and the noise echoed off the wall of trees. The cormorants rose and swam in terrible pincer towards the shore, the thirty-four of them sufficient to cordon one entire end of the inlet.

The pelicans resumed their serene approach, and when the cormorants had tightened the arc to within a metre of the shore they dived together and began to feed. Suddenly the air above the water was full of leaping mullet and skipjack, and the pelicans sailed in and scooped those breaking through the cordon.

As if on an agreed signal the pelicans retreated and the cormorants followed, and they all swam to the other side of the inlet, some still swallowing fish. The line of cormorants reformed, and they redirected their approach further up the inlet, but just as before they drew the string of their net and the pelicans kept sentry behind them. The fishing signal was given, and just as before there was synchronous diving followed by the chaos of thrashing and leaping fish trying to avoid the forty beaks hunting them.

This movement was conducted three times and then the birds left the field of battle. None flew because they were too full of fish. The cormorants swam to a tangle of marooned branches and waddled and scrabbled on to them with the cackles and mutterings of a company returning to barracks. The pelicans merely paddled into open water and began to preen or tuck their necks onto their backs and close their eyes. Baroongooba gave me the briefest glance of triumph and sailed by, the conquering general.

I'm not sure what campaign the squadron was involved in on the day when I stood irresolutely with a fish in my hand but, after scanning the river, it was clear that they were elsewhere, and so I tossed the filleted fish into the river. In winter I would save any fish scraps and dig them into the yam and pumpkin garden, but it was spring and the vegetables were planted and already showing their first leaves, the creases of their unfolding still visible.

I watched the fish float and turn with the movement of the river and, as it was close to full tide, the flow was sluggish and the fish barely moved downstream. I had taken fillets from both sides but left the stomach intact so that the air in the intestines allowed it to remain afloat, flat on the surface, one eye peeping at the sky; not a position a fish craves.

Small fingerling mullet gathered about the fish frame and began to fret and fray the skeleton. They were busy little animals, and their communal effort caused the carcass to jig and pitch despite the tiny size of the tugboats tending their big dead cousin.

Then the eel arrived, because she was covetous of any food on this part of the river. She had a small world of perhaps seventy metres at this time of her life, but it was hers and she guarded it with sinuous authority, supported by teeth like the needles of a nit comb.

She took hold of the fish's tail and jostled it against the wattle trunk that dropped into the river during the flood before last. She nudged and pushed in an attempt to loosen flesh from the frame and then she wrenched and lashed with her long body. The little mullet were not too alarmed; they'd been expecting as much and continued to work around the eel in relative safety because the amount of small fry consumed was of a quantity a proud eel scorns.

The mullets' greater concern was for the kingfisher, which was in the habit of watching such river cameos and darting in to snip a slip of silver from the water and return to its perch with the little fish flipping ineffectually. The kingfisher's beauty belied its murders.

But the kingfisher had flown upstream fifteen minutes ago

and probably would not return before dark. Did the mullet know this? Had they seen the image of the disappearing bird blurred by the water between them and felt emboldened to feed on the bream carcass dandling so temptingly on the surface?

In ponderous flight, a stingray slid beneath the jetty and rose to inspect the activity on the surface. I expected the eel to turn on the stingray and gnash at it with its fearsome teeth but the ray slid across the dead fish and the eel writhed across its back but seemed strangely cautious and deferential, perhaps nervous of the blade on the ray's tail.

The stingray repeated this manoeuvre, and each time the eel slid and coiled across its back while the fry remained unconcerned, continuing their fretting at the edges of the fish frame.

Finally the eel curved away to the murky light at the bottom of the river and disappeared. The stingray continued making passes across the fish and I could see no reason for it until I realised that it was feeding on the mullet, positioning its mouth to snip them up while they concentrated on their own meal.

The river was slow enough that I could still see the entire drama as if staged just for me. The eel, in having bunted the bream carcass to the bank, had slowed its progress even further.

Still the ray flew its solemn passage and still the mullet scattered only to reform their frittering cloud like machinists in a sweatshop.

The sky turned from lemon to rose and then brick red, with clumps of dark cloud looming like gouts of bad humour.

I couldn't take myself from the river even after the ray had left and the eel snuck back in sinuous and sullen curves to wrestle the dead fish, the water's surface darkening to the colour of gunmetal, with swatches of light like dirty silver spoons.

In this dimness I heard the first whooping and weirdly rollicking call of the nightjar. He must have roused himself from his hide among the gold and russet carpet of round-leaf box leaves where he always sleeps, invisible among the tawny doubloons.

The bird glided by me on flat wings as mysterious as the best of ghosts, dipping and curving and clipping evening insects from the air.

Soon it was too dark to see if the mullet were still feeding, and the only indications that the eel was present were the sudden nudges and bunts of the fish's body.

I left the river reluctantly and was soon absorbed in the smell of cooking and the greetings of happy dogs and the final chorus of the kookaburra. When we turn from the magic, the prosaic insists on return.

So, uncle, I write this for you because when we sat in that distant country, brought together by the intuition of your countrywoman, we talked about the land and our responsibility to love her, we talked about how in the country we were then visiting, people seemed careless of the insults they were offering to the land, their heedless abuse of the body of their mother, their arrogant teeming around her bed, the chaos of their number and the carnage of their waste.

I noticed your eyes, like clear grey lamps, and they penetrated my soul, their beautiful pearl-grey light illuminating the last secret.

Wanjiku told me you were a seer and I wondered about that, having met people who bore such a title only to find that their sagacity was largely confined to the accumulation of wealth and power.

I watched the edge of your long fingernail etch a line down the tablecloth and was brought close to tears remembering how my mother told stories with just the same illustrative tool. I was back with her, beside her final bed, as she pondered a puzzle with me. The nurses had told me she was dying, but it was hard to believe that one so active in her search for understanding could be so close to disappearance.

'Why is that black woman standing in the doorway?'

I could see no one in the doorway and assumed it was an old blind lady's dream, but she insisted that the black woman was often there and sometimes came to her bedside to straighten a blanket or smooth my mother's hair, teasing the fever from her silver crown.

Again she asked, 'Why is that black woman there? She is beautiful and kind, but I've never seen her before these last few weeks.'

But I was too busy with my own soothing benedictions: getting the washing done, holding the straw so she could drink, wiping her face with the cooling cloth, reading to her something she wanted to hear just once more.

I remember recording my own novels for her after she became blind. I built a deck on the roof of my house and recorded each manuscript onto a crumby little tape recorder. One day a shadow passed across the page, but clouds and birds often did that, so I kept reading and sometime later I took a break and looked up. There was a black-shouldered kite sitting on the television mast, barely two metres from my head. He must have been there ever since I noticed the shadow pass across the page. We stared at each other, the Wathaurong spirit bird and I, and we said nothing, but I was conscious that he had heard everything I'd written about his cousin, Bunjil, the eagle.

My mother and father had never mentioned their Aboriginality, and when I investigated the obvious discrepancies in the family history they were hardly shocked by the revelations. I wondered about their lack of surprise, but it was in her final months that my mother began seeing black women through her blind eyes.

I was distracted by the need to lace myself up against grief, so I avoided the strange woman's presence, saving my attention for the old frail woman I loved so much, the woman whose conversation I still crave.

On her last afternoon the nurses were worried and tried to prepare me for the worst. My mother was sat up in her bed and entertained her remaining sisters and the friends gathered to grieve for this woman of frightening intellect and relentless compassion. They came to mourn a woman who had held them up, kept them from stumbling in their darkest hours, but she refused to let them mourn; she told jokes, and invoked gorgeous flowers grown in her garden before she'd become blind and those she had smelt and touched since. She argued that she could still see them simply by allowing her finger to trace their petals with that long storytelling fingernail, a crooked blade that had become yellow and horny, the colour of a cicada husk, a brittle, cloudy amber.

I had to leave the bedside because there were too many others pressing around her. There was not one square foot where another person could stand. Nurses hovered briefly in the doorway before giving up and leaving. Nothing they could do was more important than to leave those final words uninterrupted. They too had come to love this fragile old seer.

I left the door open and watered the pot plants she'd asked me to bring so that she could 'see' them from her bed. Her voice carolled in the room and people laughed and she stoked their laughter with her undiminished understanding of how to warm and coddle the heart of another.

When they'd all gone and the sun was almost finished, she asked, 'Did the robin come today?'

'No, Mum, the robin didn't come. I think she was jealous.'

'That's a pity,' she said, but then raised herself a little and looked past me. 'Hullo,' she murmured, and turned briefly to me, adding, 'The black woman is here,' by way of explanation for one who was clearly not sufficiently perceptive to realise the woman had arrived.

My mother continued to stare as if in silent communication with her last visitor and then slowly lowered herself to the pillow, and her open eyes saw the ceiling. 'I wonder who she is.'

They were almost the last words she spoke. The evening became a watchful solace and the forehead-mopping and hair-smoothing metronomic but increasingly edged with agitation.

Who was the woman by the door?

Well, uncle, of all the people I've met, I believe it was Wanjiku. Perhaps it is my desperation to want the ghostly woman to have been the equal of my mother, someone with her fierce intelligence and towering grace. Perhaps I'm wishing for my mother a companion on the journey whom she could ask the questions I was too dim and fretful to answer.

My mother's death seemed an incredible waste. Her mind was still edged like a scalpel, her back strong, her legs capable of pacing the corridor, and yet other unseen elements expired. The air was suddenly empty of meaning. It made me remember fishing on the great elbow of the Jinoor River from which I could see the hooked peak of the mountain. I was drifting downstream with fishing rods mildly resting on the stern when a feather wafted by my face. A moment before I had heard a quiet *thwack*, as if someone had hit a tea towel with a pencil. I looked up and there were several more feathers floating towards my face. I was transfixed, but in the presence of the mountain and the fecund smell of salt on the river, I was often taken by this mood, and turned my gaze back to the rods and stared at the bank where bream spines flared as a fish wrenched mussels from the submerged rocks.

Someone hit the cloth with a pencil again and this time I was aware of the blur above me as the peregrine warped and the feathers again drifted about me; the feathers of a swallow. I held my palm upwards so one could land there, the midnight blue sheen tinged with the red of a sunset cliff. I stared at the feather in thrall, my witness to one small horror in the world's daily turn.

That's how I felt in my mother's empty room.

Uncle, I hope you don't think it presumptuous of me to dare tell *you* a story, but my mother made me, and by the time I saw your fingernail and eyes, time had diluted my memory of that last day. Well, as you can see, I've forgotten very little, but it has become like a stone above the searching lips of the tide to which a light rain or dawn dew restores colour, brightens and glosses what has become dull and dry.

It is like watching the feather settle in the palm of my hand.

So thank you, uncle, and thank you, Wanjiku.

I'm not sure I can explain the parable of the stingray and the eel except perhaps to guess that it's the glorious inevitability that follows the drawing of breath.

In my culture, having listened to your story and told one in return, I have become obliged to you and your kin. I would do whatever I could in your defence or for your comfort. Even if it was just to stand in your doorway.

PRIMARY COLOURS

You never expect it. It's like being eaten by a shark. It does happen, and people shed their redness on the waves, but it will never be from your waist that the shark snaps a morsel of kidney fat.

So here's Jackson, digging a row of fence post holes a mile long. The notch on the spade handle tells him when to stop digging. The string line and divot tell him where to start. Pleasantly hard work. Unpleasant oceans of mind-free time.

He looks out over the waving spring grass of the paddock and admires the lush growth of rye, clovers, paspalum and fescue. He helped the earth yield this fine pasture, and in the middle of the paddock are the follies. The grove of banksias he couldn't cut down. The tuft of scrub around the wombat-hole and several thickets for the resting place of travelling birds. And everywhere, single, fine, clean trunks of white gums, right down to the forest by the creek. Jackson's Folly. The hardest paddock to plough in East Gippsland, but the only one with resident kingfishers, eagles, emus, nightjars, bandicoots, snipe and ducks.

His heart takes in the flight of the cuckoo-shrike, the sweep of the swallow and the tracks of kangaroo, snake and dingo. This is his heart's place, and here at his feet is his heart's blood.

His daughter. He can see her red hair hidden in the dark green clover, and the kelpie's tail waves above the grass uncertainly. They are stalking each other. Suddenly they leap out, and she shrieks. The dog carouses, with short barks, and they tumble in the grass, delighting in a long deliberate roll to the bottom of the hill. They're both mad, both mates.

They play like this every day while Jackson slams the crowbar into clay. Each morning when they arrive, the dog courses the playing field, checking for black snakes. There are none anymore; their smells have staked out the place.

His back has had it. He could split a hundred posts a day and dig sixty holes. Feel like an Anzac. Fall the tree, billet the log, bark the billets, split the posts, dig the holes, tamp the post, run the wire, hang the gate on corner posts the tractor can't lift. And now? All for nothing. It's over. The selection, the vow – down the drain. Mistakes.

The shadow of his favourite white gum tells him it's half an hour past lunch, and he calls to the two ginger pelts. The dog leaps through the grass with her back curved like a whippet, the tongue everywhere, the eyes ecstatic. The girl comes tumbling after, shouting, screaming with joy, the hair a nest of lovely copper, the arms flinging with the delicious energy of a young animal.

Jackson's mood is set by the plunge of the bar, the gouge of the spade, the lift and tip of the earth, and the wound of his thoughts. The metronome is invaded by the two rampant beasts who tumble and screech, upsetting sandwiches and themselves.

She loves this. She doles out the food and drinks. Jackson gets his own coffee because she can't lift the steel thermos, but she pours her cordial and hands out the dog's biscuits, which the kelpie eats like a 'good dog', enjoying the ceremony as much as the girl.

Jackson sits with his back to the old white gum, girl and dog draped on him, the remnants of lunch in disorder around them. He watches the movement in the grass as wood ducks waddle down to the creek, and he sees Van Gogh's waving grasses, the wind making patterns on the nap of green plush while the kingfisher sings at the nest. God is surely in His heaven, but this man struggles to cap off his tear ducts.

'Rain, Dad! It's gunna rain.' Dog and daughter are up, searching the perfect blue sky. He mumbles about the ducks shaking water off their feathers as they fly by, but it doesn't matter – lunch is over, the frolic has begun.

There are the beautiful primary colours. Absolute azure in the sky, the rich green of the grass and the red of dog's tail and child's hair. His heart surges with the beauty.

The crowbar wavers, the spade stops shovelling. Jackson packs up the tools and calls to the gambollers in the grass. They collect a few stones, shout out down the wombat burrow a few times, look for four-leaf clovers, collect petrified wood from up by the tractor and play in the grass. A formula for daily bliss.

They bound after him through the grass. Down at Duck Hole the blackies quack and ogle and paddle off to the further end, and father and daughter strip off, watched by the dog, who isn't so keen on the swimming bit.

Daughter sits on the little jetty while Jackson swims a slow length in the icy water. He glides with his head just above the surface, and the ducks allow him to come among them, ogling with stupid alarm. *Goodness, goodness, look at that!*

The girl has the big tractor tube ready when he swims back, and together they paddle about the pond while the kelpie is frantic on the bank.

Apricot glows above the trees, and more ducks and cormorants fly in while they dress.

Walking up the hill, the evening settles like the murmur of a woman's voice, and yellow robins sing the end of the day. The lyrebird clicks in the scrub as they plod on to home.

Home.

Smoke straggles away from the chimney, the generator chugs, they can even smell things cooking. Daughter dashes in, tugging stones and cicada shells out of her pockets as she goes.

The kelpie and Jackson bring in the cow to the little bark-roofed bail. The jersey chomps away at the oats and rolls her huge dark eyes. Those eyes, with their long lover's lashes. Jackson presses his face into her side and the cow takes a step to spread her weight. Milk drills into the tin bucket and in the rhythm of this lovely flesh-flesh movement, both are content. Ease for her, milk for him. He breathes in her lovely cow smell and watches the sky flooding with vermilion behind the trees. The yellow robin is piping its last message, the cormorant plops into the dam, and the world closes its day with such careless grandeur. Ten million such symphonies, and each time such sad, beautiful, perfect joy.

Jackson stands with the bucket and releases the jersey. She presses her oaty muzzle against his leg as she ambles off to her calf. The man looks up to the house on the hill, lights aglow in the window, smoke a mauve smudge from the chimney and a full bucket of milk. What could be more perfect? Perfect.

PITTOSPORUM

Sometimes there is violence.

I could blame the pittosporum, but that wouldn't be right, although it was the end of summer and the air was thick with it. But it wasn't that, because pittosporum induces a dolorous lassitude, a luxurious and passive ease.

I remember one night at a party I smelt it in a room, above the smoke and powder and spilt drinks, people's clammy shirts, smoked oysters trodden into the carpet. I searched the room expecting perhaps a vase on the mantelpiece or a Vegemite jar on the fridge, but no, it was in a woman's hair. She was beautiful enough. Well built, those summery Australian shoulders; you could imagine your lips grazing the clavicle. But I just reached up and took a lungful of the flower. Took her by the shoulders and turned her head towards me. Bit abrupt, you might say, but hardly violence.

'Why the flower?' I asked her.

'Oh, I passed a tree and thought how pretty it was.'

I nodded. I could imagine her in the street, graceful with summer's langour, lifting a lovely arm to pluck a stem of warm liquor.

Now, for a man with not one decent line of introduction, you'd think I'd stumbled on the great opening gambit. I mean, she was surprised, but she hadn't turned away, and her lips were parted waiting for me to explain an interest in flowers ... and why I still had my hands on her shoulders.

But she had the voice of a woman whose mind had difficulty distinguishing amour from Armani. One mention of the seduction of pittosporum and she'd giggle. I smelt the flower once more, released her shoulders and left. Of course, half the room looked on me as a man from whom you'd expect violence, so I stumbled from the house and straight into the embrace of the pittosporum night. It makes you drunk, I'm sure. The backbone goes as soft as a fresh stem of tulip, the mind unaccountably blurred.

But you can't blame the pittosporum.

The Yarra River at Fairfield is very beautiful, and in one spot it has cut the shape of a huge horseshoe, a natural amphitheatre where in more innocent days they'd built boatsheds, tearooms and a wonky old swimming pool in the shade of the willows. My father learnt to swim there, and later I swam in this pool with my cousins. You can see why I'm well disposed to the place, but when the woman I loved got the job as producer of *Medea and Lysistrata* to be staged by the river, I was ambivalent. You could see straightaway it would be an outrageous success. You knew it wouldn't rain, you knew the Greek chorus would be drowned out by cicadas, and the natural inclination of people to breathe in the fragrant air would glaze them over with thoughts of love. People would never forget the time they saw *Medea and Lysistrata* at Fairfield even though they'd heard maybe a dozen words all evening. Well, how many words of *Lysistrata* do you need? Have you ever read it? It depends on an audience clubbed into equanimity by retsina – or flowers.

So, when I was asked to do the backstage, I was hesitant. I hated seeing the bleachers bolted down onto a glade of family memory, but then my love had asked me and I was drowned in the pools of her eyes, enmeshed in the blonde skeins of her hair, so I said yes. I knew it would be a success and I knew it would be a magic few summers' nights that could be spent in a childhood haunt near the one I loved.

On the night in question, the opening night, I stood on the hill as the people began to arrive, ambling down the terraces, tossing their heads when they laughed, their teeth flashing in moonlight and footlights. The warm air, the lazy U-bend of the dark river and, of course, the pittosporum had fucked them all. Women could feel it between their thighs; men had an inclination to yawn and nuzzle their girlfriends. The whole night conspired for romance, women's arms seeming always on the point of lifting to rest on a shoulder, fingers to idly curl a strand of hair, so men noticed the tug on their scalp, and eyes would meet and you know – ah, yes, pittosporum. It was like a scene from *A Midsummer Night's Dream*, a play within a play, the audience behaving as if the drama was all theirs, they'd thought of the jokes spontaneously, that very moment, each idle gesture to be remarked upon by a theatre critic next morning.

It was the magic dusk when *A Midsummer Night's Dream* works best. We were doing *Lysistrata*, but it didn't matter. Bud lights glittered in trees like cicada eyes, and the stage was a confection of nonsense, someone's drawing board of dreams propped up against the real thing. People knew they were in for an entertainment and were already laughing for the froth and bubble they were to see.

Yes, the pittosporum had drugged them. Fucked them with flowers. Just the mood you need to watch *Lysistrata*.

Actors from stage and screen strode about the boards saying

improbable things, engaging in bits of bawdy pantomime to a willing audience. Oh, he's had his bum whacked with a bit of board.
What fun! Oh, look, she's got a pillow up her dress. How droll. Of
course, the cicadas saved us all from the interminable dialogues of
pomp and power.

Backstage, all I can hear are the portentous creaks of chipboard
and pine as famous feet ham it up beneath the dark and soughing
trees. I stand with my back to the flats as women tear off one lovely
gown to tug on another. I look across the onyx bevel of the river
trying not to think about love slipping from my hand.

The main actress returns after a strident competition with the
cicadas to which the audience was well disposed. Everybody defers
to her because she's famous and her name is on all the billboards,
but it has to be said that she's no Rhodes scholar. Of course, this
hasn't deterred her male co-star, because he's in love with her in
the way that stars fall in love with other stars. This means he has
spent the best part of a fortnight faxing the production office on
the hour and mooning about at rehearsals, trying not to catch the
eye of the comedians, most of whom appear regularly on a TV
show with the sock puppets and fluffy ostrich.

Outside, in the night air, with a real river lapping at its banks
a metre from the lighting box, it's hard to take the theatre seriously.
It's so obvious that all of us are real people striving to overcome our
disbelief that we are other people.

But the actress is ready, and I have to help her climb the ladder so we can hide in a chipboard box from which she will make
her final, cataclysmic cicada speech. We've had to do the ladder five
times because she doesn't like it, and I've begun not to like her, so
that lifting her gowns and steadying her feet as she ascends to our

hide is not a calendar event. In the box we stare into each other's eyes, listening for the cue which we hope to hear in between cicadas and the slapping of plywood swords, because six or seven intricate things have to be done with ropes and bodices, hinges and crowns. It's a nightmare. The director should be shot.

Twice we think we hear the cue, but it's only an actor searching for the right line and another retrieving a cue for the second time. They get it right just as I notice the actress has lost her slipper. Now, it could be a moment, like the girl with the pittosporum in her hair, where I reach and secure the silver shoe on the queen's foot while our faces are centimetres apart and her hand is on my shoulder – but we stopped liking each other at ladder attempt number three.

Her eyes see the shoe go on and say thanks, you saved me, but that's all, and off she goes to be Medea and confuse the cicadas with talk about Olympus and a chariot full of other gods. When she finishes, the audience goes ape, and actors chuck wigs, ply and paste into a corner and go off to be hugged by the insiders, showered with flowers like real Olympians while we, at the back, pack boxes and sort out tackle.

Later, I go up to the dressing tents to compare notes with the director and to see how we've ruined his art this particular night. The comedians sit around in steamer chairs, drinking cans of beer and gazing sardonically on the people as they pick their summer selves up off the terraces and out into the park.

The producers and investors are an excitable bunch of councillors, doctors' wives and Greek travel agents who plunge glasses of champagne down their necks and laugh into each others' faces knowing that they're onto a winner, knowing they won't have to deny they had anything to do with *Lysistrata* by the river.

And she is there talking to a Sydney friend. He's the man who casts all the movies and miniseries. Beautifully dressed, a haircut you can't get in Coburg, a look of intelligence and breeding in his eyes, and she is engaged in earnest, astute theatre-type conversation with him, and everything tells me not to allow my lumpen self to approach this tête-à-tête.

Do trout eat old worms? Do salmon eat mangled and smelly whitebait? Do businessmen fall under trains? My feet approached and she cast me a glance, not of disdain or dismissal, but of what appeared like despair. As though she wanted me to be cooler, smarter, better dressed, capable of social interaction beyond the plaintive look and the gruff hello. But whatever skills I'd ever possessed in this area had leached away during that fifteen minutes in a chipboard box waiting for the actress to risk herself on the eggshell balcony and the jerry-rigged ropes of her harness. The shoe was the last straw; if she'd stumbled once she would have plunged to a quick death for herself and an early bump out for the rest of us. It wasn't the time to comment that we'd saved a fortune in insurance by not mentioning her name on the policy. My clothes had absorbed a gallon of sweat while I prayed the star with the modest voice and tremendous cleavage wouldn't die in a tangle of my ropes and hardware.

I wasn't in the mood for love by the time I climbed down that bloody ladder, but the slinking river, the sigh of leaves, the aching scent of pittosporum made me clumsily, bloodhoundedly intent on a declaration.

The casting agent cast one look at my damp shirt and knew that no wardrobe department in the land could dress a bunch of limbs like mine. He left, and we, she and I, were face to face. She wouldn't look at me, so I reached out my hand.

Here comes the violence.

She gathered a jacket and bag and marched off in brittle strides to the car park. I should have let her go, but does a trout eat worms? I was fascinated by the bait. I crunched across the gravel like a portent and reached her just as she opened the door of her car.

I took her right arm below the elbow after missing her hand and said, Please.

Please what, you'll all say, but it was just please: please don't get in the car, please turn to me, please succumb to the pittosporum and drape your arms around my neck as all the other lovely arms in the park are slender about the necks and waists of their men.

But she just gritted her teeth in unendurable frustration and tried to draw her arm away, and me, oxen-dumb, my hooves digging into gravel, resisting.

You're hurting my arm, she said.

Please, please, I said, don't go.

This was stupid. Under no circumstances could this plea work, nothing could be more assured of driving her away, but still I clung, and at last she tugged her arm free and I saw the white print of my blunt claw and then the door shut, the car reversed away and I was left in a night strung with stars, murmurous with the whispers of lovers, as warm as the inside of a woman's elbow and saturated with the perfume of sweet flowers.

But what does that mean to an ox, or a trout, or a salmon? What do they know about starlight, warm flesh and perfume? No, it's just us, the brute and violent people, who know anything about pittosporum and have to suffer its irresistible promise.

STAFF DINING

for Aunty Barbara, Aunty Cath and the brothers of the interior

I f you split yellow stringybark you get a remarkably clean, flat face, but inevitably, several knots intrude on the plane, evidence of branches fallen in the tree's history.

In this case there are two small, almost horizontal knots for the eyes and a narrow, recessed split for a mouth made mean by ignorance. A cruel, unnecessary thing to say, you might think, but there's confusion in those squinty pits, a constant bafflement at the small, difficult matters of life. And there's been a trauma. An accident as a child, a pinched nerve, a stepfather wanting to erase evidence of his paramour's first love.

The face flinches once or twice every minute, and that quick grimace seems to compound the confusion, a terrible accumulation of doubt that makes his hand reach down to caress his certainty, a bunch of large, brass keys, smoothed with use.

The staff dining room seems to specialise in big, gruff men, refining the Australian idea of masculinity to a stern contempt. One massif. The belly a solid rising plain, jaw jutting above it like a crag likely to defy crampons, pitons and ice axe. He's been adzed

from wind-exposed manna gum, the trunk so writhen by gale that
when split by blade a slab is hewn on a tight curve, giving the face
a perpetual twist of distaste. Or hatred. Because the escarpment of
his mountain is both tall and wide, it is necessary for his arms to
be held a little away from the body and the hands to loll with the
knuckles facing forward. This is so, not because I want to invent
a brute, but because I saw a man whose arms are simian. Does he
have more keys than everyone else, or is their jut made more threat-
ening for bristling beneath such a glowering cliff?

And then there's sallow wood. It's a blond, waxy timber that
splits nicely to a clean, well-modelled face. Perfumed, too, like
vanilla or a summer night when gardenias exhale. But should you
paint two unblinking eyes on that wood, it is a betrayal of the sweet
timber. If those steady eyes level at yours with their controlled stare,
you feel as if the pretty wood has decided that all others are criminal, beneath and beyond the courtesy of empathy. Do not burn
sallow wood for warmth.

So many of the timbers here are like this, as if repressed rage
has kilned them hard and sapless, as if a million locomotives have
hammered the grain of the sleeper to tight resistance.

Well, whatever the case, they have a thing about doors. They
like to hear them slam. Shut. The door is designed for positive closure. Steel on steel. Clang.

One, maybe two, hold the door so that it can ease into place. Still
secure, still shut, but silent. More or less. All the others, especially
those with the more prominent keys, the more impassive slabs of face
and mind, seem to take comfort in the clang. Shut. Positive closure.

We are waiting in the timber museum, readying ourselves,
pretending to have enjoyed our free lunch of ham croquettes, the

shape and texture of a pitbull's turd. Three days old. No warmth and a dry, resistant crust. Hand grenades are more palatable and less dangerous. The cook responsible reminds you of Swelter from the Gormenghast kitchen. Your glance must land on him for less than the blink of an eye, for he condemns your gaze, punishes candour with another hand grenade. Keep your head down.

Is all this gruff neo-violence just the guard of the guard, or are they recruited for being in possession of a visage capable of turning blooded beings into stone or salt?

We have plenty of time to observe this room. We are invited to remain there for approximately ninety-seven minutes. We are intimidated by the percussive blast. Perhaps it is meant that we should be. Blackfellas. Free blackfellas. The worst kind.

Aunt is a wallaby. Solitary. Alert. Steady gaze intent above the grass. Watchful but easily alarmed. Black wallabies stay alive due to their intelligent vigilance. Aunt is alive. But I see pain in her face with each blast of the vicious door. It tells her something that causes her to flinch. Simon shields himself with an impassive, watchful face, and Muk Muk – well, he resents the restrictions, the dumb cynicism, and you can see Bolshevism brewing beneath his pastel-knitted beanie, glowering like a furious gumnut baby.

We look down. Wait. For release. To visit those for whom there is no release, just the heavy smoothed key turned by a knotted hand. These other men are so nakedly blooded, so tenderly fleshed, so vulnerable to the wounds from eye and mind. They look away from the timbered face, fighting with their pride and defiance. *Look away. Look away. Don't meet that eye or you will fall as a sparrow in a meek flutter of feathered breast and curling claws. Look away, my brothers, Medusa doesn't specialise in stone here, she enjoys clumps of spent feathers and the excuse to extinguish the brave. Look away, my brothers.*

Slab points to a door as if it might be our abattoir, but inside there is no evidence of blocks waiting for the axe. Every wall is covered by paintings: Maori, Chinese, Fijian, Samoan and ours. Plain old blackfella. There are Maori warriors with moko and weapons held across their chests; Fijians with aggressive tongues and murderous eyes; Buddha, inscrutably calm but depicted against the Great Wall from which the Chinese fought the hordes with lance and sword.

And the blackfellas, what do they do? Do they grimace or scowl or threaten the throats of lambs who dare? No, they plait baskets, kick footballs, offer their fists cushioned by gloves; they dance, befeathered by colourful birds. It breaks your heart to see the peace of our people: the mildness of our hope, the sweetness of our defiance.

Sweetness, Bookman? Surely you're gilding the lily. Admirably loyal, but misleading, don't you think? Well, no, even though our boys are clad in the bottle green of their penitence, our difference is in the gentle finning of our cross-hatched fish, the brolga still warmly tucked and folded in the egg, blue wrens screenprinted on a shirt, a man's shirt, the sweet gaze of the kangaroo. Yes, sweet, lashes long and girlish, batting above the eyes of does.

We value different things. Unfledged birds within the egg are no match for haka or the fish hook carved from the bone of a Maori slave who has it explained to him by the cousin who cut his leg off that when he gouges the eye into that hook with a gimlet, it is his eye, the slave's eye, so that when the shark takes the hook, his leg bone, he will see deep into the mouth of his consummation.

No, we are different. This is not to boast, compare or deride, but to explain how we in this country think of different things. When allowed.

We have left the lumber yard of impassive flitches and have entered the singing forest. We are surrounded by art. How could it be any different? Today it is just our boys. Koorie Day. We watch as twenty different brushes draw colour in unerring lines. Fish, kangaroo, echidna, brolga, wren. We are different.

Alan is silent, his face downcast, but even at that angle you can see him struggling with emotion, as if nursing a great sorrow, a deep regret. He's razored a fine paintbrush to within two bristles of extinction, and with whispering caress paints a meticulous grid on the soul of a barramundi. For four days he does not look up from that quiet concentration except to lean on his elbow and stare at his fish or draw those two bristles through his tight lips, sharpening the accuracy of his intent.

'My mother is dead,' he says at last, in answer to a question I have not asked.

Brad has a scar across his shaven skull that stretches from ear to ear, and another old injury that has crimped one eye so that the pupil glints from beneath the damaged lid. It's not a face you want to meet for the first time after dark.

We're supposed to be teaching writing, but they are painting in such deep peace, only malice or paternalism would ask them to attend to anything else.

Aunt, arms akimbo, but heart still exposed, leans across to him. 'That is gorgeous, my brother.' The look of alarm and doubt that crosses his face would make any Aboriginal cringe with the knowledge of that doubt, the knowledge that sometimes such compliments, such acknowledgement, is often accompanied by an intervention or an Act that requires you to disown your cousin. I know that look, my brother, and I know that Aunt will not let you live with the doubt. And before I've finished wishing her to smooth the feathers of the startled owl, she touches his arm and says, 'Truly, my brother, it is beautiful.'

And I see that other look pass across his wounded face, because I know it well, feel it on my own, which is why I pick up a brush as if its brand is of great interest to me. I dread that he might cry. If that's what men did.

Len sits beside me, toying with a brush, as if he too is fascinated by logos and quality. He passes things to other artists: tracing paper, paints, cups of tea, cotton-covered boards. And then he sits back and watches. Silent, but his face open, young, a tic of eagerness at the corner of his eyes and lips.

At last he dips a brush into a pot of umber and paints one single straight line directly on the table, as if he's been reading too much about Giotto.

I stare at the line. He lays down his brush. 'It's true what you said, Uncle, yesterday. We talked about it last night. We are learning our culture. We want to learn. We're sick of this shit. We want to become good men.'

I stare at the brush through glimmering eyes, too afraid to look up unless I do that thing men do not do. I touch his sleeve instead. 'Too late, my brother, you already are.'

Anthony brings a cup of tea. Every day a cup of tea, and for a single teabag they have to queue and look penitent.

'I had a dream, Unc, last night, it happens a lot, nearly every night. Bunjil comes down and picks me up in his talons and carries me over the wall. And when I wake up and find it's not true

I ... you know I'm ... Do you think it's true, Unc?'

'Bunjil will come, my brother, he always does. Bunjil never holds a grudge. You wait, bruz, he'll take you over the wall.'

He reaches under the table to grip my hand because we've been told not to touch. 'Thanks, Unc,' he says. 'I believe you.'

We don't look at each other. Boys don't. And neither of us sweats from the eyes because we don't do that either.

I glance at Aunt. The watchful wallaby has become a crouched owl, puffing feathers on a branch. This might be the hall of bright carvings, but it's cold and it's got into her bones. A young man is seated at her elbow and his beanie is pulled so low across his brow you can see but half of his irises. Two owls crouched on a branch, murmuring about the long night. She catches my eye in one owlish glance and I can see that her fellow bird's lanced pain has crept down her throat and gripped her windpipe.

I've seen it a dozen times before. They seek her out. For her calm acceptance, the way she'll flay her heart to ease theirs.

I look at the owls in awe. How did he know to fly to this branch? And what horrid story has he told her? I'll never know because it's not mine to know. He flew to her branch and she'll never give a hoot.

I love you, my brothers, and Aunt ... well, you know what I'd do for you ... put a foam bead on the frame of that canteen door. To stop the final clang that some slabs enjoy.

Leaving the hall of bright carvings to recover our belts and biros and coins, I find it hard to re-enter the other world, of blank and careless wood.

I turn once more to the aviary door, reluctant to leave its feathered hope. Restful sleep, my owls of the great forest. Blink a little if you must, but wake restored.

THE GALAPAGOS DUCT

Medical textbooks tell us that the Galapagos Duct is a cranial passage with a conduit to the brain and connected to the organs of both ear and eye. Fluids within the aural canal can negotiate the Galapagos Duct and influence the brain's reception and transmission of aural and visual stimuli.

This conduit's connection to all three organs provides the opportunity to render the inexplicable explainable. It is an intelligence moderator.

Take a little thing, like how in 1493 Pope Alexander VI stamped a piece of metal, announcing his authority for the edict that deemed the discovery of lands presumed the right of the discoverer to dominate the savages living within that land. Savages were defined as those who did not believe in the Carpenter of Palestine.

Now, we have had frequent opportunities over centuries to read this document written on calf skin and to speak about it with our priests and princes. It has been acknowledged by men of the law, blessed, sanctified, assumed into law so that it has diffused in the liquid of the Galapagos Duct, and from there it has seeped into the crimped and slippery labyrinths of the brain.

There are a great many Catholics and lawyers, so this knowledge has seeped into the minds of our rulers, many of whom have been, or are, either Catholics or lawyers. In fact, combined, they would be a clear majority in our legislative chambers. You can imagine the amount of seeping going on, the trickling up. So we know that we know what the Pope said. We know that assumption of others' land was related directly to the Christian religion.

Vegemite, however, causes an imbalance in the fluid of the Galapagos Duct. It encourages unnatural spaces to open between the cells, and a disconnection occurs so that information within the duct is not properly received or is held for too little time in the cranial chamber.

Advanced science produces many outstanding results, and a small laboratory in Lakemba, Sydney, has identified the ingredient in Vegemite that interrupts the workings of the Galapagos Canal: beer. We know that Vegemite is made from the dregs of brewing, but until the work of the Lakemba chemists we didn't know that the hypersalts of beer production could cause such dramatic effects. The disconnection means that we lapse into a yeasty dream when it comes to listening to the complaints of the subjugated peoples. 'Sorry, what did you say? I was dozing.' The subjugated population repeats itself, but once again the Galapagos Duct interruption victim says again, 'Sorry, what did you say? I've just had a Vegemite sandwich. I'm a bit sleepy.'

Galapogas Duct Interruption Syndrome (GDIS) is so powerful that it can eliminate entirely the remembrance of death or suffering. Not for GDIS sufferers; their pain is still felt exquisitely in the body and brain. It is the suffering of others that drifts into a distant memory, so distant that the GDIS sufferer guffaws when the savage complains about her death.

Crucially, because the GDIS sufferer is a Christian, inheritor of the papal bull, he feels charity for the dead and damaged, and so reads books about it in the reading room of his colonial cottage in a leafy suburb identical in almost every respect to the one in an English leafy suburb, which, freakishly, is also called Kew. And of course the books are written by sufferers of GDIS.

The delusion is caused by the failure of the Galapagos Duct. Under delusion, the sufferer witnessing a lack of education or appalling health is likely to call in the army as a remedy: dispossess the sick and uneducated, take away all their support systems, and deride the authority of their Elders – call them paedophiles, for instance. The GDIS sufferer is likely to call the imposition of this trauma a justified intervention, a necessary punishment.

The least likely response to any Indigenous problem will be to examine the facts of the cultural history. The GDIS sufferer avoids any exposure to the knowledge that land was stolen from a fully functioning society, the longest living culture on earth, the birthplace of social development. He or she will run screaming from the fact that the oldest villages on earth have been found in Australia. They will avoid the inconvenient truth that fish traps at Brewarrina are probably the oldest human constructions on earth, that a midden at Warrnambool is as old as 120,000 years, 50,000 years earlier than the time at which the Out of Africa theory suggests humans first left Africa. They will consider it a nuisance that the oldest ground-edge axe in the world was manufactured in Western Australia 50,000 years ago, and feel no sympathy that the proponent of this discovery, American ethnographer Norman Tindale, was laughed out of the country by Australian archaeologists. They will meet with paternal incredulity those who suggest that in light of recent archaeological finds, bread was likely invented by a woman at Kakadu 65,000 years ago.

The GDIS sufferer remembers none of this, and still mows his lawns in Kew and Kensington, comfortable – smug, you might say – in his belief that he 'inherited' a land from a people innocent of any civilised quality.

*   *   *

So profound are the effects of GDIS, and so soporific, that when Vegemite is removed from the diet and the interruptive agent in the Galapagos Duct is diffused, the sufferer may begin to hear the plaints of the dispossessed and a point of enlightenment may pierce the mists.

As the environment worsens, resources are depleted and capitalism collapses – as it almost did during the global financial crisis, under the weight of those calamities and the opportunism of stupidity of adversarial politics – we will search frantically for a solution, a straw to clutch in order to stop us from drowning.

Inevitably we will turn our eyes back to the earth. We might gnash our teeth for a few more years as we live on our reserves and blame the poor, blacks and Muslims for this state of affairs. Eventually we will have to admit that we depend on the earth and not the reverse. Hopefully we will agree that our predicament was caused by the hubris of the Bible, a hubris that deemed the earth was simply there for our wasteful domination, and that all humans were ripe for domination because we declared the Christian European to be God-like and all others savages.

When in panic of the looming peril we turn to the skills of the First Peoples, we might look at the economic system that survived in Australia through millennia. We will find the grains and tubers that, due to having been domesticated in this land, need no more water or fertiliser than the land provides.

Most of the grains are gluten-free and most of the tubers do not produce sugar but fructans, a gentle substance that promotes digestion and robust health, as the first European adventurers noticed.

We will turn back to these plants not because we regret the invasion and are trying to make recompense; we will turn to them because we must, because they will represent the necessary elements of our survival. Then, perhaps, we might begin to wonder how to ensure our survival as a nation, and we might wonder what form of social development will protect our precarious existence.

We might look to Aboriginal governance. If we consider that governance and become familiar with its age, complexity and persistence over time, adopted generation after generation by young people who were convinced of its intrinsic fairness, we will wonder at the massive philosophical achievement of those old, patient minds who insisted that a good society would ensure that everybody is housed, everybody can participate in the culture, and everybody, when old and frail, will be loved, supported and listened to by the young.

And we will realise that the world's most profound philosophical statement, *bingyadyun gnallu birrung nudjarn jungarung,* is replicated exactly in the earth, rises from that earth, and that it includes us as a component, not a conqueror, as a modest deliberator, not a dominator.

LEFT-HANDED WOMAN

There's a woman at Cape Otway and I can't get her out of my head. I think of her every day. I know what she eats, I know what she looks at when she wakes each morning. I know the most intimate things about her. I know that she is left-handed. I know that she is meticulous, and I'm sure she has a son. I know all these things, but I dearly want to know what she thinks.

I discovered her bedroom and kitchen and, like a thief turning over the contents of her drawers, I began to know her secrets, the things only lovers and family should know. I am ashamed, but men under thrall do not always act with honour.

Is she beautiful? Her aunty certainly was. I've seen a photograph of her. The mischief in her eyes, even at eighty. But the woman of my fascination is probably more discreet, or at least I imagine her so. Because of her things, how she goes about her life. Or is that the romantic notion of a man under her spell, a man aching to see her, to ask her just one question, to look into her eyes, if even for the briefest moment?

What right do I have to dare crave this woman's attention, to lie awake at night wondering about her? My claim on her is that she is an Australian and so am I. We have both slept, loved and eaten within sight, sound and smell of the bay she saw every morning. She is my countrywoman. Dead now, murdered, but if we had met we would have been able to talk tides and fishing, fruiting and waterproof seams.

You see, I found where she slept, where she cooked, where she sewed her winter clothes, discovered that she was left-handed, and her son too, most probably. On the Cape Otway cliffs in the longest unbroken occupation site in the world I found her seamstress's kit. I saw that she had five different needle sizes in two different shapes and could dress the end and edge of her needles to keep them in perfect order so that the seam she sewed was completely waterproof. And when I went to use her implements I also discovered she was left-handed.

Later I found her son's hammer and axe. Well, I am only guessing that they were her son's, but given the incidence of left-handedness in any human population and that the man and woman lived at the same time, the chances are they were mother and son. He was also a meticulous craftsman. The hammer he made from a piece of limestone is among the most beautiful objects I've ever handled. But it is not as beautiful as his mother's sewing kit. This is no bigger than a matchbox, but on the two flat surfaces there are graded holes, grooves and notches to hone needles, cut thongs and yarns and dress needle points. The person who made it was deft and proud. I can imagine her heart filling with pride at her ability to care and provide for those she loved. She was proud, beautiful and left-handed.

It was information of a far too intimate nature for a stranger to know. I turned and looked out over the view from her doorway and sat down almost involuntarily, shocked that I had entered such a private zone. The tide was going out and revealing the pools where she had gathered her crayfish, abalone, skutus, urchin, sea lettuce, sweep and whiting. I knew that already because I too had fished there and taken home the same bounty so I could sit at my table among my family and feel proud. I used her recipes: the chargrilled rock lobster, the sweep stuffed with peppercress and bower spinach, the abalone poached on coals with sea rocket and bush-pepper garnish, echidna and yam in the earth oven cooked to perfection in Lomandra baskets resting between clay heat beads.

It was impossible that my countrymen and women could find this most womanly of women inhuman. The failure to understand that this woman could bake and sew and keep a neat home, provide for her children and be true to her husband, and most of all know and love her country, binds me and my fellow Australians in the grip of an ignorance she never knew.

I wake at night dreaming that I could take food from that woman's hands. Take the food she offered me; not her land.

PUBLICATION DETAILS

Versions of the following stories have appeared in the previous publications: 'An Enemy of the People' (as 'Elbows on the Bar'), 'Franks Is Dead', 'Left-Handed Woman' and 'True Hunters' in Bruce Pascoe, *Convincing Ground: Learning to Fall in Love with Your Country*, Aboriginal Studies Press, 2007; 'Andrew Bolt's Disappointment' in *Griffith Review*, no. 36, Winter 2012; 'Big Yengo' in *Griffith Review*, no. 42, 2013; 'Choosing' in *Review of Australian Fiction*, vol. 2, no. 1, 2012; Sections of 'Here Is a Story I'd Like You to Tell' (as 'Smiling in the Dark') in Andrew Rule (ed.), *Man and Beast*, Melbourne University Press, 2016; 'Honeypot Two Shots Two Pots and Miss Hermansberg' in Anne-Marie Smith (ed.), *Culture Is . . . : Australian Stories Across Cultures, An Anthology*, Wakefield Press, 2008; 'Lament for Three Hands' in *Southerly*, vol. 71, no. 2, 2011; 'Peaceable Kingdom' in *Southerly* online, 19 September 2016; 'Pittosporum' and 'The Bridge Near Nowa Nowa' in Bruce Pascoe, *Nightjar*, Seaglass Books, 2000; 'Primary Colours', 'Soldier Goes to Ground' and 'Thylacine' in Bruce Pascoe, *Night Animals*, Penguin Books, 1986; 'Reaping Seeds of Discontent' in *3010: Melbourne University Magazine*, issue 2, 2016; 'Rearranging the Dead Cat' in *Southerly*, vol. 71, no. 2, 2011; 'Rene of Rainbird Creek' in *Meanjin*, vol. 65, no. 4, 2006; 'Sea Wolves' (an edited version of the 2016 Lin Onus Oration given at the University of Melbourne) in *Island*, no. 149, 2017; 'Temper Democratic, Bias Australian' (an edited version of the 2017 Stephen Murray-Smith Memorial Lecture given at the State Library of Victoria) in *Meanjin*, vol. 77, no. 3, Spring 2018; 'The Headless Horsemen of the Drummer' in *Meanjin*, vol. 68, no. 2, 2009; 'The Imperial Mind' in *Griffith Review*, no. 60, 2018; 'Too Upsetting' in *The Monthly*, July 2016; 'Water Harvest' in Bruce Pascoe, *Dark Emu*, Magabala Books, 2014.